YOUR FUTURE IS CALLING

YOUR FUTURE IS CALLING

MIKE ECHOLS, PH.D.

HUMAN CAPITAL LLC
Omaha, NE

Internet website addresses and links within cited websites are regularly updated and subject to change in address and navigation. That's the nature of our technology and can cause frustration for readers.

Download the separate chapters here: http://futureiscalling.com/

Cataloging in Publication Data on file with Publisher

Design and production: Concierge Marketing Inc.
Printed in the United States of America.

This edition last updated September 2016.

10 9 8 7 6 5 4 3 2

CONTENTS

One of the most emotional moments in my life occurred in 2008 inside a Home Depot store. I was pushing an empty shopping cart around the aisles of the store to exercise a healing broken leg. The healing was an appropriate metaphor for what I was about to experience.

As I turned down one aisle, I saw five young men and women in their orange aprons talking among themselves. In one explosive instant I saw a complete picture of them as they were in that moment. But even more clearly, I saw the potential for a more fulfilling life. It was an emotional response that came from knowing about the opportunity that a very special program would have in improving the quality of their lives. The stage for that special moment of recognition had been set a few years earlier.

In the mid-2000s I led a team of educators from Bellevue University in the creation of a strategic relationship with the senior management of The Home Depot. Jointly we developed an education program using The Home Depot employee tuition assistance benefit to pay employee college tuition costs.

To all of those individuals I have touched in their quests to create better futures for themselves and their loved ones. Education has paved the road to those futures.

PREFACE

All Home Depot employees are eligible, but they must be willing to invest themselves in this leadership development degree program. At The Home Depot, employees "opt in," meaning the employee, not the company, decides whether to invest the time and energy to enroll and learn. This was not a training program; it was a college degree program.

Our challenge was to convince management that this joint effort was good for the company as well as the employee. In the end we accomplished this, but there was a Bellevue University chapter to this story before the program was launched.

Months before the program was implemented, I was engaged in discussions with Bellevue University's Program Planning Committee to secure university support for the university investment required. I could see some of the challenges ahead. Academic personnel are not the most innovative members of our society.

During those deliberations, an academic leader told me that he would not support the initiative. He believed that the average employee at The Home Depot was not a good candidate for a college education. I knew he was wrong.

You see, I am the son of an eighth-grade-educated East Texas pipe-liner. Not a single member of my family had ever attended college before I did. My academic colleague believed that Home Depot employees could not do what I had done. In other words, the possibility of the better future I obtained after graduating from college was beyond the reach of these men and women. He implied that they could not be successful in completing a college-degree program.

Eventually I received the necessary academic approval for this innovative Home Depot program. We launched it in 2005, and many Home Depot employees have enrolled. Since then, several have been promoted to senior leadership positions. These motivated employees showed everyone that they could earn their degrees.

But this book is not about academic programs, companies, or even degrees. It is about you. It is about what you need to know to create a better future for yourself and your loved ones. It's about re-committing to getting the education you need to have the future you desire.

The journey you are about to embark on has the potential to create a future in which you look forward to your workday. The joy in your new future is the result of doing what fulfills you, not the result of doing something because you must merely "make a living."

To be successful, you need a clear vision to guide you in your journey and help you decide which path to take at each fork in the road. This vision must also inspire, motivate, and, above all, sustain you. In the end it will be your passion for the future you are creating for yourself that will determine this future.

Will it be easy? No. As you work on making a better future, you will be distracted from your vision. Your senses will be bombarded by subconscious appeals to your emotions. Your mind and body will be tempted to surrender to the future others are trying to impose on you.

This is because the less your current life fits who you are, the greater your stress and exhaustion. Intense negative emotions can divert you from your path to a better future. When this happens, your path is hijacked by the emotions of today. It is easier to give in to the exhaustion of the present and give up on the possibility of a better future. In this instance, doing nothing is the greatest danger to completing your journey and changing your future. Remember, if you are not taking the next step, you will never get there.

In the end, it will be your passion and your emotional connection to your vision of the future that will sustain you. Your hunger and thirst for a better life will keep you on the path to success and prevent you from getting side tracked by the negative emotions you encounter when you are exhausted by pressure and stress.

In this book I lay out a road map for you. This road map has many forks in the road where you'll need to make a decision. The content is chock full of information, suggestions, and examples to assist you in making the choices that align with your vision.

What you need to make this future possible is here. But in the end *you* have to weigh the information and choose because this journey is about who *you* are and what *you* do, and not about who I am and what I do. I can be a mentor to you, but I cannot make the choices for you. You must do that.

This book is my offering to you of the possibility of a better future. My hope is that it will spur you to get the education you need to compete in the twenty-first-century global economy and create a better future for yourself and for your loved ones. The possibilities are endless. My wish is that you use the information, guidance, and support in this book to empower you to that future.

Does this program work for the employees it was designed to help? Have they created a better future for themselves and their loved ones? Yes. Here are some testimonials to that fact:

- "I have been able to use everything I have learned throughout the program in my current role as a district manager and wish this was something that was available sooner in my retail career." DG, The Home Depot

- "This program allowed me to spend time with my son. The classes have given me confidence." PK

- "It all has shown me 'why' we do things. I have been able to share much of the information with my team and I feel it has truly helped me grow as a leader." CW, The Home Depot

These comments demonstrate the drive these adult learners had to complete this road map to a better future. To these individuals I say: "Thank you one and all."

Now—it's *your* turn!

CAREER + EDUCATION –> YOUR FUTURE

The most important decision you will ever make about your future is completing your college degree. This book is packed with information to help you make that decision and create your valuable future. Where that information is and how to use it is available here simply for the reading.

A decision to give up on your degree will put you at a severe competitive disadvantage for the new jobs of the future. Even today 60 percent of the jobs posted on the online job site http://www.Monster.com require bachelor's degrees. If you don't have a bachelor's degree, the majority of new career opportunities will pass you by. The job situation will only get worse in the future.

Not everyone is convinced. Some argue that a college degree is not necessary to have a successful and prosperous life. Those people point to Bill Gates, Steve Jobs, Oracle's Larry Ellison, and Facebook's Mark Zuckerberg as highly successful individuals. They are. What they all have in common is that they were college dropouts. They started and then left their college programs. They all walked off campus and never returned as a student.

The careers of these celebrity business leaders are powerful evidence that it's not necessary to have a college degree to be successful. You can be successful without one. But that's the exception not the rule.

But the question for you is not whether that kind of success is possible, but whether it is likely. Here again the evidence is clear. The best chance that you have for a better job, more personal satisfaction, and more income and security for yourself and your loved ones is by completing your bachelor's degree.

Although it is possible that you could win the lottery, a few people do win at Powerball and get all of the millions that go with it. But every time a Powerball lottery is paid out to a handful of winners, there are tens of millions of players who did not win. You never hear about them. For those losing-ticket holders the loss is acceptable because a lottery ticket costs only a few bucks. When you don't win, you are out the cost of a latte from Starbucks and it's easy to say, "Oh well, maybe next time."

But the college degree completion decision is not like playing the lottery. You can lose a lot more than the price of a cup of coffee. Degree completion takes your money, time, and energy. It is a decision not to be taken lightly.

So here is a challenge for you. Ask yourself this question:

"IS A COLLEGE DEGREE WORTH IT?"

The answer is absolutely yes. But it is a sure thing only if you make the right choices in the beginning, not after you go to an expensive college and leave with tens of thousands of dollars in student debt.

Here is the deal about this book. The debate about "Is a college degree worth it?" is over. The answer is yes with the right decisions now. This book is about helping you make sure that the answer is yes before you invest tons of money, time, and energy to earn your degree. The two key words to look at are *worth* and *it*.

The *worth* is about what you will have once you have completed your studies and are awarded your degree. At a minimum you will have a piece of paper that you can hang on the wall as a trophy to be admired. You will deserve all it represents. But in the end it will always be just a trophy. That trophy alone will not feed your kids or put a roof over your head. Only what you learn can do these things.

Trophies are important in what they represent. Your degree will be a valuable symbol. It broadcasts to the rest of the world your intelligence, energy, and success.

The real worth of your degree is in what it empowers you to do—what it makes possible. Here is the most important thing you need to know about the *worth* part of this conversation. Not all degrees are equal. In fact, many are nearly worthless when it comes to what they make possible for you and your loved ones to do. If the particular degree you select fails to make possible what is valuable *to you*, it is virtually *worthless*.

This is true no matter how fancy the diploma or prestigious the institution awarding it. This is about you. This is precisely why this book begins in chapter 3 with a look at who you are.

If your degree completion efforts put you into a career that fails to fit "who you are," the pursuit of that degree will have been a terrible mistake. Your future depends on making well-informed decisions today.

The best decision for you requires the absolute best facts. This important information is available in this book in chapter 7, How to Pick the Right Career for You, and chapter 8, Where the Jobs Are – Today and Tomorrow.

Don't pick a college major without reading them. Without this information it is highly likely that you might take on $30,000 of student debt (the current average) and earn a worthless degree.

Pick wisely based on good information about who you are and career opportunities your choices create.

So not all degrees are automatically "worth it." The choices you make today have a direct impact on what your degree will make possible for you in the future.

The second part of your decision is about the *it* in "Is a college degree worth it?" The *it* in the phrase "worth it" refers to the time and money it takes you to earn the degree. This is about the investment that you will make in your education. If done wisely, this decision can turn out to be the very best investment you will ever make. If done poorly, this decision can lead to student debt that imposes a tremendous financial burden on your future.

Student debt is a huge issue for all of us. That debt can be the personal financial burden that delays home ownership, family formation, and other important life decisions. Huge debt at such a young age is an economic cancer. It has the potential to be a destructive force rather than the valuable investment it has the potential to be. Your choices determine which of these futures are in store for you.

So this brings us back to the question so often being asked today: "Is a college degree worth it?" The answer is no when you select a path that requires student debt so large, you'll never be able to repay your loans.

You have one overriding investment objective. Your goal is to make the cost of your degree as low as possible given who you are and what career is best for you. Your are challenge is to secure and evaluate the information you need to make a good decision. I can assure you the information is out there. You just have to know where to find the data and learn how to use the information to your advantage.

There are many good ways to reduce cost. The key is to have the information you need *before* you select a college or university to attend, not after you have already enrolled.

To reduce the cost you need to know the actual cost of the tuition to attend the college of your choice. I can confidently tell you that the tuition cost listed on the college's web page is not the cost that the vast majority of students actually pay to attend that school.

The real cost of tuition varies greatly from college to college. Important information on the actual tuition paid at American colleges and universities is available from Tuition Tracker, http://www.tuitiontracker.org. My one hard piece of advice to you is this: do not, under any circumstances, agree to attend any college without first getting the actual tuition costs for that college on http://www.tuitiontracker.org. You should do this work for every college you are considering attending. You have tens of thousands of dollars at stake.

Another important fact is the credit transfer policy of the university you are considering. For valuable selection and financial information, see chapter 9, How to Pick the Right School, and chapter 11, How to Pay for College.

In the end, if you do your homework here, I can almost guarantee you that the answer to the question, "Is a college degree worth it?" will be yes. But for that guarantee to apply to you, you need solid information. Without your effort before you enroll, you might as well take your coffee money and buy a lottery ticket.

Some Americans make that choice as the path to their future. It is the wish and hope path. When that happens, you can wind up with a worthless degree and huge student debt. Your future is too important to treat it like a lottery.

But it is a sure thing only if you make the right choices in the beginning, not after you go to an expensive college and leave with tens of thousands of dollars in student debt.

■　　■　　■

02

IS A COLLEGE DEGREE WORTH IT?

You may be surprised to know that almost 40 million Americans have some college credit but have not finished their degrees. I call them dormant students or inactive adult learners. You may be one of them. If you are, this book has important advice to help you get the right degree for you along the most efficient path possible.

If you are a military veteran, there is information here for you too. And even if you don't have any college credit, but you think you need a degree, this book is for you.

Unfortunately, for many adults, it often takes a negative event or life-changing experience to nudge you in the direction of pursuing or finishing a degree. Those "aha" events might be getting fired from a job, passed over for a promotion, or laid off; death of a spouse; divorce; change in household income; children getting older; or children starting school.

Some event usually triggers that decision to return to school. Regardless of the motivator, the good news is that higher education is available to you, especially if you're committed to reaching your personal goals and being the best you can be.

Your commitment might include the following:

- Getting the right information about schools and programs
- Having a realistic strategy to reach your goal
- Being able to reprioritize your resources (time and money)
- Facing and overcoming obstacles (time, money, and fear of failure)

And having the courage to stay the course.

Today, many people ask, "Is a college education worth it?" However, the real question should be, "Why does a college education that is so important to all of our futures have to cost so much?"

Cost and value are two different things. The fact is that a degree has never been more valuable, but, without better decisions, it has the potential to cost too much. So is a degree worth it? The compelling answer is yes.

The good news is that the majority of high school graduates (and virtually every nontraditional student who never finished a degree) has the potential to earn a degree.

But wait. According to data released by the U.S. Census Bureau in December 2010, only 28 percent of Americans have earned a bachelor's degree—even though potentially more are able to. In our high-tech marketplace, this gap is creating shortages of needed skills and shortages of degree holders.

Even in the face of high unemployment, the staffing organization Staffing Talk asks the question: "Why are there 4.5 million unfilled job openings in America today?" The answer is that there is a tremendous mismatch in the job market today. Not enough people with degrees to fill jobs. Is one of those jobs waiting for you?

The outlook presents us with both good and bad news. The bad news for our economy is that the lack of educated citizens is approaching crisis proportions. The good news is that if you get your degree you will move into a market where forecasts say demand will be greater than supply. And when demand exceeds supply, the price goes up.

In this kind of job market, prices are the wages and salaries employers are willing to pay you. There are too few students who will earn college degrees, and those who do earn them are not obtaining the skills that are in demand. This is important for your future and will be addressed in great detail in chapter 7: How to Pick the Right Career for You.

The United States of America needs you to return to school. Once you become a degree holder, those laws of supply and demand work heavily in your favor. An educator, researcher, and entrepreneur, Vivek Wadhwa of Duke University, explains, "China and India are educating. If we're going to dumb down America at the same time the world is getting smarter, we'll become a Third World country."

Your opportunity is to be a part of the much-needed supply in a career the world needs.

WHAT'S HOLDING YOU BACK?

Since you already have an interest in going back to school, you intuitively understand the value of an earned degree. Maybe you have been waiting for the right set of circumstances or an external push from a loved one to finish your degree. I know that people take a break from their education for many reasons. The most common include lack of time, money, or interest or becoming a caregiver for small children, aging parents, or a sick family member.

Not surprisingly, the same issues that cause students to abandon their pursuit of a college degree are often the same ones that keep them from returning to their education. Children need attention and care. An aging mother moves in. Your job takes up most of your day, and there just doesn't seem to be money left over at the end of a paycheck.

In other cases the underlying issue preventing nontraditional students from finishing a degree is their own self-doubt. Adult learners can be paralyzed by focusing on questions that create further doubt such as these:

- *Will I be able to really do it this time? Am I smart enough?*
- *Is this program the right place and right pace for my current lifestyle?*
- *Will I be able to find the financial resources?*

Self-doubt is often the result of having dropped out of school once before. The fear of having to drop out a second time in the future is real. In some cases the doubt is so severe that returning students purposefully hide the fact that they are back in school when they do decide to return.

What will help you reach your personal education goals is not what you doubt but what you *want*. It is about who you want to *be*. It is your strong vision of the future you are creating for yourself and your family that will sustain you. It is your personal commitment to yourself and your dreams that will allow you to stay the course.

Also needed is a renewed sense that you will not get lost (again) on the way to your degree. You cannot afford to take a wrong turn at this stage in your life. Instead, you need a road map with clear directions to give you the confidence to always take the next step on your journey. This book is that road map. It contains clear directions on what to do next to complete your passage to your degree.

BEGIN AT THE BEGINNING

Your personal journey is important. It is okay to look up to others who have already made their journey. They serve as role models and can provide inspiration. But in the end, where you are going and the future you are creating for yourself and your loved ones is about you. It's not about them.

This is about gathering information and evaluating your options at each step. When you look back, you will see how your path differed from the paths of others. Right now it is important to get on the right road at the beginning.

One key to any successful journey is to understand where to begin. It sounds so simple. The temptation exists to "just get started." Surrendering to these impulses is a big mistake. The time and energy you spend at the beginning to understand where you are starting from will be invaluable to you over time. In this journey you begin with "who you are." For now, it is important to reemphasize that the starting point is a critical part of any successful journey.

Another critical aspect to every successful journey comes from knowing where you are trying to go. I know this sounds obvious. In this journey the destination is about you and who you intend to become. The destination is about what you will do every day in your life five, ten, twenty years from now. It's about *your* future and the future of your loved ones. Only you can create the vision of what you want to do with your life. It is this vision that will sustain, fulfill, satisfy, and give you the things in your life that fit who you are.

FIND YOUR PATH

For every adult learner, there is a path to finally earning your degree. Along that path there are mountains and valleys, and the journey is filled with excitement and frustration, ups and downs, disappointment and success. It may seem like a long journey today but with the right choices it can be done.

As a road map, this book will help you chart that journey to stay the course. It will provide valuable information that fits your journey and your future. More importantly, it will simplify the process and help you make the journey one step at a time. This is a long journey involving reliable information about careers, income potential, daily activities, and colleges and universities. The journey is overwhelming without a road map with directions on what you need to do next.

At the beginning of the journey, your brighter future may appear to be far, far away. It does for everyone. It did for me when I was making the journey to earn my degrees. However, the key is to get started on the right path and from there have the information you need to take that next step.

Each separate chapter in this book provides important information along with step-by-step guidance on what to consider next. Each chapter alone provides important information and guidance for your decision, but the greatest benefit to you comes from the entire book. By linking together the guidance in each chapter, you will be able to lay out a complete path through the maze to your future.

Without this road map it is easy to feel defeated even before you begin. With the road map, you can make each turn and select each alternative with confidence that you have the best information necessary to progress toward your goal.

I know the very thought of returning to school can be daunting. It certainly was for me when I returned to school after being in industry. The task is complicated. We all lead busy lives with many responsibilities, including other people who depend on us. The notion of adding one more thing to your to-do list often feels overwhelming. The obstacles seem unnerving once you add in the challenges of finding the financial resources, choosing the right field of study and school, and becoming more disciplined in time management.

Going back to school involves a drastic reallocation of time, priorities, and commitments. It's especially taxing for the growing number of people who live away from family and close friends, who could otherwise help with balancing family obligations. While the road may be difficult, it is possible for you to complete your degree.

Like a mentor, this book will inspire you, hold you accountable, and make sure you have packed the right resources for the journey. In addition to this book, you need to surround yourself with real-life mentors too. The chances of your success are vastly improved by having access to people from whom you can learn. They have journeyed on their personal paths and can give you wise advice that will be important to your success.

Not surprisingly, research shows that people who have strong ties to those who have already completed their degrees are more likely to complete a degree themselves. Once you are enrolled, it takes discipline, organization, time management, focus, patience, humility, sacrifice, hard work, dedication, and sheer determination.

For adults with jobs and families, it requires a support system of people who can shoulder some of the responsibilities that you may no longer have time to perform. Staying the course will take flexibility on the part of you (the student), the school, employers, and family members. In the end the outcome is worth the sacrifice.

In my role at Bellevue University I've seen nontraditional students complete their degrees time and time again in recent years. In fact, I have dedicated this book to them and their quest. To these individuals I say, "Thank you one and all."

Now it's your turn. I believe you are up to the task. So what are you waiting for? Your future is calling.

■　　■　　■

03

ENVISION YOUR FUTURE

Earning your degree on the way to your purposeful future consists of a series of steps, decisions, exercises, and activities. These will take you from where you are today to where you want to be in the future. Each chapter links to the next, so the greatest benefit is in reading the entire book and doing all the exercises.

Creating your vision is critical. This vision needs to be identified at the very beginning of the journey. Your vision is the beacon for your journey. It guides your passage. It informs your next step. It inspires you. It energizes, motivates, and sustains you. Your vision of your future needs to be both clear and powerful.

In the end, your vision of your desired future is not the end of your journey, but instead the most critical item you need at every step during your journey. When the journey gets difficult, which it will, your vision of your future will be your primary source of energy that keeps you on your path and that inspires you to take that all-important next step. Your vision will help you determine your priorities and the resources needed to persevere, regardless of the barriers that inevitably appear along the way.

The goal of this chapter is to help you create your vision, assess where you are today, and begin formulating your road map for the journey to your future. As we go through the process together, remember, the initial goal is not to write a "to-do" list, but rather to create a "to-be" list. In other words, focus on this question: What do I want my future to be?

DOING THE WORK

Once you have made up your mind to earn your degree, there is a temptation to "just do it." Americans are especially vulnerable to the appeal of taking action, including me. But I want to caution you not to give in to this temptation. Now more than ever it is critical that you take the time and invest the energy to gather information, consider your options, and, above all, set off in the right direction from the beginning.

It helps to put the initial activities in perspective. You need to take your time and think about the exercises and data in this book. The temptation is to do otherwise.

Here's a story about an experiment with two test groups of people. Each group is asked to open a sealed box with a computer inside. The experiment requires the subjects to use the computer. One group was composed of Japanese citizens, and the second group was American citizens. How these two groups carried out their assignment was very revealing and ultimately relevant to the decision you will make using this book.

The Japanese test group opened the box and took out the computer and the instruction manual. Then they placed the computer back in the box and set it aside. They proceeded by reading the instruction manual from cover to cover. Once complete, they put the manual down, took the computer back out of the box, and only then did they begin to use it.

By contrast—as you might have guessed by now—the American test subjects took the computer out of the box, put the instruction manual back in the box, plugged the power cord into the back of the computer, pressed the ON switch, and waited for the system to boot up the home screen. As soon as the computer booted up, the American subjects were on the keyboard, typing. The instruction manual only reemerged if and when the test subjects got stuck.

For the Japanese subjects the manual was the first resort. For the American subjects the instruction manual was the last resort.

This story illustrates an important point for your journey. As Americans, we have little patience for the instruction manual. We just want to "get on with it." For many, instruction manuals are for getting answers after we encounter a problem, not as a wise way to get information before trying it (whatever "it" is) in the first place.

The American cultural bias toward "getting on with it" has advantages and disadvantages. The good news is that we are action oriented and willing to take chances.

Here's an example that relates to college: Pick a school. Take some general education undergraduate courses. Postpone selecting a major. Then select a major. Later, change to another major. Sound familiar?

This is the path many young high school graduates take in their first attempt at a college degree. This process often results in the accumulation of plenty of credits but no degree. In fact, in this scenario, students take courses and use this time to figure out what the end goal will be. The hope is that the future right for them will emerge from the classes they take along the way. Most often it doesn't happen. Does this sound familiar? This is one of the reasons there are nearly 40 million former college students without degrees today.

Today's adult student can't afford to "figure it out" as he or she goes. College is just too expensive today. You do not have the luxury of endlessly exploring degrees and majors in the hope that you will eventually "figure it out."

My advice to you is to "figure it out" before you begin studying specific subject matter or selecting your major. The investment you make before you enroll (or re-enroll) in higher education will be far more productive than simply jumping in and beginning to take courses without a plan.

A DAY IN THE LIFE OF YOUR FUTURE

Your vision of your future needs to be more than an abstract dream resurrected in peaceful moments of daydreaming. It has to be an ever present resource in your daily life. It has to be something almost tangible to you. Your vision has to be so real you might even be able to touch it, feel it, and experience it as though you are living it today. It has to inspire and motivate you. It has to be ever present, not periodically summoned when all else is failing. It cannot be a last resort. It must be a first priority.

Your vision must be so powerfully linked to your future for it to compete for energy in your life every day. It competes against the intense and real feelings and priorities of your current life. Your life every day creates strong feelings, thoughts, and emotions. The demands of the kids, the stress of the job, and the concerns about the future are present in your daily life.

On a practical level, your vision of your better future competes against your daily emotions when it is time to sit down and do the work that will lead to your degree. To stay the course, your vision of your desired future has to be strong enough to enable you to rise above the demands of every "today."

If your vision of your future doesn't successfully compete with the demands of your daily life, you will not have the stamina to take the next step needed to complete this journey. The more compelling your vision, the more motivated you will be to embrace your journey. That's why it is important to take time to reflect and envision yourself in your desired future. The only limits are those of your own imagination and the energy you are willing to invest to develop that vision.

Need additional inspiration? I suggest reading biographies of people you admire such as George Washington, Abraham Lincoln, Susan B. Anthony, John Adams, Andrew Jackson, and Ben Franklin. Or consider Oprah Winfrey, Jack Welch, Lee Iacocca, Billy Graham, or, more recently, Steve Jobs.

When people write biographies about others or autobiographies about themselves, they often include personal accounts of achieving dreams as well as overcoming major obstacles and roadblocks they encountered along the way. Many successful people learned to endure great difficulties along their journeys. These often include neglect, childhood abuse, chronic illness, or severe poverty.

Just think how Oprah's story exemplifies this arc of triumph over tragedy. The inspiring model Oprah creates is rooted in childhood poverty. She was abused as a child and functioned in a largely male culture. Yet in spite of all these handicaps she has risen above them. She has created a compelling future, not only for herself, but also for the millions she has touched. She is a mentor worth following.

A common theme among many of our past and present heroes—the people we have come to admire and respect—is that they came from humble backgrounds. They were raised by parents who never dreamed of attending college and were often unable to offer any significant career advice to their own children. As different as these people might seem, one attribute they have in common is a strong internal drive to create the life for themselves that they envisioned.

If you are fortunate enough to have such role models or virtual mentors in your life, they can provide you with the inspiration you need to continue on your personal journey to a better future. If you don't have role models or mentors, seek them out. They will become a very important part of your team.

Practically speaking, for adults with demanding schedules, it is especially critical to create a vision of the future that aligns closely with areas of interest that bring you satisfaction. To help you here, let me give a little lesson on the structure of a bachelor's degree in America. Such degrees are made up of three main components:

1. General education (gen ed): Such courses as history, social sciences, English, and some math. The gen ed core is required to earn a regionally accredited degree in America.

2. Major: The major is about the particular skills associated with your degree. The actual degree will be something like a Bachelor of Science degree with a major in physics.

3. Electives: Your college or university will define what qualifies as credit-worthy electives, but the choices are really vast and can be very appealing.

Avoid elective subjects and majors that are not personally fulfilling. Professors may require many assignments you don't enjoy. When this happens, you will associate your course of study with drudgery, which is the death knell for all learners. Don't unnecessarily impose these obstacles on yourself. They make your journey difficult and tiresome, and, eventually, they will drain the motivation you need to complete your degree.

Whatever vision you create, recognize that staying the course and sustaining your commitment are some of the toughest challenges you will face. That's because as an adult learner, you will have many demands upon your time and energy—demands from employers, children, family members, and significant others.

Begin your journey by acknowledging and building on your current strengths, talents, skills, and interests. If you focus on the positive, the sacrifices you make along the way will seem easier to deal with. Start by finding the time to pause and reflect about a typical day in your life.

What activities make up your typical day? Take the time now to write them down.

- What activities do you look forward to?
- What activities do you wish someone else would take care of?
- In the course of your typical day, when do you feel most satisfied?
- What types of activities seem to generate their own energy and inspiration?
- Which activities leave you feeling drained, spent, and exhausted?
- What do people tell you that you are naturally good at?
- What activities would you really like to be doing every day in your future?
- What are some activities you see others doing that you would like to be doing in your own life?

The answers to these and other questions will help guide you in creating your vision. So do it now. Your vision must be firmly established before you take the next step on your journey.

SELF-ASSESSMENT

The approach that is often used to obtain a degree starts with choosing a college and then selecting a major. Next, individuals focus on getting a job and then, not until much later, do they try to figure out what leads to long-term satisfaction in a career and in life. My advice and the foundation for this book is the following: do it in reverse. It all starts with who you are and the other decisions follow from that starting point. Then pursue your major at a college.

Know yourself. Even though it may be a challenge to find the time, invest in an honest self-assessment of where you are today and where you envision yourself tomorrow. A self-assessment involves performing a critical analysis of your goals, interests, skills, and experience. It also identifies your strengths and weaknesses by evaluating your accomplishments to date, in both your personal and your professional life.

Of course, many of us prefer to spend more time reflecting upon our strengths. It is a lot more satisfying and far less difficult. But knowing our weaknesses is strength in itself. When you are aware of your weaknesses, you can think about and compensate for them so that you are better prepared when your less developed skills are called into action.

This assessment process is fundamental to your journey and will determine what tools and resources you will need along the way. It is crucial to approach this process with complete honesty from the very beginning.

Research paints an unfortunate truth about self-assessment. Often people use self-assessments as tools to validate their own beliefs. Feedback that supports your beliefs may feel good in the moment, but it does little to help you with the important decisions you need to make.

This difficulty in honest self-assessment was revealed in research conducted by Dr. Constantine Sedikides, director of the Center for Research on Self and Identity at the University of Southampton. Through scientific research Sedikides aimed to better understand the roles of self-evaluation methods in terms of self-verification, self-enhancement or true self-assessment. In a series of four experiments, he discovered that subjects tended to favor self-evaluation questions that verify, rather than assess, their own self-knowledge or self-concept. This confirmed the notion that true self-assessment is more difficult to obtain than self-verification or self-enhancement, since participants are not naturally objective.

However, in a fifth experiment, he told his subjects explicitly to approach the questions objectively, as if they were approaching their self-concept as a scientist might, by bringing each trait under close scrutiny. Subsequently, the subjects appeared to be objective, and the questions strove more for accuracy rather than verification.

Some questions to consider as you begin your self-assessment are these:

- What are my strengths and weaknesses?
- Do I work better alone or with others?
- What would my mentor say are my natural talents?
- Am I better at math, reading, or science?
- What subjects have I struggled with in the past?
- What subjects have I excelled at in the past?

Other self-assessment options include creating a list of personal attributes such as these:

- I have the ability to work with numbers.
- My communication skills are excellent.
- I'm a whiz with organizing things.
- My people skills are first rate.
- I have good common sense.

It's also helpful to reflect on your educational background and professional experience to examine what personal abilities contributed to your success in relation to the demands of these roles.

Closely examine what you have accomplished in your life. Make a list of activities you performed in each of your former roles. Record what you were really good at and what you enjoyed. Also look at hobbies and outside interests to reveal where your passions really lie and how they inspire your future.

In any case, here's a word to the wise. This is not the time for self-deception. If you kid yourself, you'll complicate your journey and create obstacles that stand between you and the successful attainment of your dreams.

INVENTORY YOUR PERSONAL ASSETS

Now that you have completed your self-assessment, gather your personal "assets." You will need them for your journey to earning a college degree. These assets will determine how much time, energy, and money you will need to invest to earn your degree. This is the time to

- Order all transcripts from previous colleges.
- Inventory and record all learning experiences including your employment, volunteer work, and military service.
- Gather all former entrance test scores and certificates earned.
- Ask your employer about tuition assistance benefits.

The assets you have collected make you unique. What do I mean? Have you ever watched the Antiques Roadshow? It opens with ordinary people standing in line carrying one or more personal items patiently waiting to see an expert and discover the value of their treasured items. The items range from old books, pictures, rugs, paintings, posters, toys, crystal, silver, porcelain figurines, and rifles to interesting family heirlooms.

Selected individuals are invited to sit with an expert and discuss the items they brought to the show. They enthusiastically share where the item came from and how it came to be theirs. After the story, the expert joins in telling their story as it relates to history, where the item originated, the era of its creation, the creator of the item, and sometimes who originally owned the article. All of this is important. It establishes how much the item is worth. But it also gives the owner a more complete sense of what they have. Various experts may value the same object differently.

What does a family heirloom have to do with your education? Lots.

First, as a nontraditional student, you are as distinctive as each item presented to the experts on the Antiques Roadshow. Your transcripts, test scores, certificates, learning, and work and volunteer experiences make you distinct. These are the treasures you bring to the show. At the same time, you are uniquely qualified. Evaluating your value, however, won't be easy and will depend on which colleges you decide to apply to (more on that in chapter 9, How to Pick the Right School).

The "currency" of college is accredited credits per semester hour. Typically, 120 semester credit hours are required to earn a bachelor's degree in America. To the average person, all credit hours may seem equal, but this is not the case in higher education. What one institution will accept as a credit hour toward its degree requirements may not be accepted elsewhere. It is important to realize that the value of what you have will depend somewhat on which college or university does the evaluation—just like on the Antiques Roadshow. Every institution will evaluate you independently.

Ultimately you will make a college choice. In the meantime, it's more important to look in general terms at what you have today and what you need to have in the future in order to achieve the future you desire. We will soon see that selecting the right university is one of the last choices, not the first, as has traditionally been the case.

INEXPENSIVE TOOLS THAT HELP YOU FIND OUT "WHO YOU ARE"

We're all different. That's obvious. Just look at us. From our appearances alone, it is clear that no two of us are exactly alike. Your journey starts here—with who you are.

But who are you? That's not so obvious from the outside. When we look inside each of us, the differences are much less apparent but in the end are far more important than skin tone, eye color, or how much hair we have or don't have.

Scientific research tells us that what is on the inside—who we are—is formed early in our lives. Research by Dr. Donald Clifton at the University of Nebraska explored the theme that our brain makes favored connections quite early in childhood. His research points to these neural connections in our brains that determine "who we are" throughout the rest of life.

Oh, no doubt we also learn throughout life, but this early formed brain structure fundamentally establishes who you are. The journey you are on now actually began when you were very young.

Many people go through life trying to discover who they are one step after another. This approach is very costly in both time and money. This universal quest is revealed with such comments as these:

- The forty-five-year-old who says, "When I figure out what I am going to do with my life ..." Or "When I get a real job ..."
- The college student who enrolls at a college with the mission, "I want to find myself."
- Or the retiring adult who wistfully says, "I wish I had ..." Or, saddest of all, "If I had it all to do over again, I would ..."

You don't have to spend a fortune on a college education that does not satisfy you or spend your life literally stumbling from one experience to another trying to figure out who you are. There are no guarantees, but there are some efficient ways to get your answer to this important question.

Again we turn to scientific research for useful answers. They are highly effective and take little of your time and money to use.

These tools are not meant to change who you are. They are not about learning to make you better or developing skills needed for employment. They are about one simple learning experience. They are meant to help you learn who you are. They do so in a straight-forward, logical fashion.

Here's how it works: You answer private questions about what you like and don't like. You provide answers to well-structured questions that map your personal responses to a profile. From the profile your answers are mapped to careers that have the potential to guide you to a productive and fulfilling career.

One last comment before I get into specifics. Whether you use these scientific resources is completely up to you. For whatever the reason, you may decide to do what millions before you have done—namely, figure it out for yourself.

For better or worse this is exactly the path that I have traveled in my life. I am living proof that it can be done. By the grace of God my life has worked out to be this wonderful experience. Yours can be too. It's possible. My only message is that there are easier and more efficient ways to travel this path. New resources are available. At least look at them and then make up your mind.

So let's take a look at the scientific research-based tools and assessment instruments for measuring who you are.

For those seeking a new career or a career change I recommend that you consider the Strong report iStartStrong available at the parent company CPP website www.cpp.com. The tool helps provide a map between your personality profile and the careers available in the real economy. With that, let's get to the specifics of the Strong Interest Inventory.

For our discussion here, you can expect some of these outcomes from this assessment. The company describes the tool like this:

Designed to be used as a self-service instrument, the iStartStrong™ report puts self-discovery into the hands of anyone seeking career direction, re-entering the workplace, or seeking more satisfying work within an organization. Based on results from the world's most respected career assessment tool, the Strong Interest Inventory® assessment, this personalized report paints a picture of how one's interests and themes link to various jobs, work settings, and career fields.

One of the features that I particularly like about this instrument is that it calibrates the Strong Interest Inventory. But this instrument goes beyond who you are by translating your interests to the career opportunities that fit who you are. It does this by mapping from your interests to careers on O*NET. I talk in much greater depth about the O*NET database in chapters that follow this one.

The cost of the iStartStrong instrument was $9.95 in 2014 and is well worth the expenditure. Simply follow the instructions on the CPP website www.cpp.com.

This chapter brings more insight into why this self-discovery is so important and so valuable to defining the future you desire. After all, this journey is about you and starts by using valuable scientifically based information that efficiently calibrates your interests.

FILL IN THE SKILLS GAPS

Skill gaps between where you are today and your desired future are normal. In fact, some returning students are lacking in one or more of the essential skills needed for learning. The essential skills are math, reading, and writing. These skills are essential because they are fundamental building blocks to learning the skills of your major. You cannot function on a team or solve problems without these skills. But not having these essential skills at the beginning of your career journey does not have to stop you.

There are excellent online tools available for your use if you are willing to use available tools to help you gain those skills early in your journey. Whether your shortcoming is in math, writing, or even reading comprehension, by identifying your areas of weakness you can take the action steps necessary and address them in order of priority. There is no shame in needing to gain new skills to contribute to your journey.

Certain fields of study, often called "the major," require special skills and talents. To illustrate, fields such as technology and engineering require learning that develops in sequential order and builds from one level to the next. Using a different example, calculus requires prior study in foundational mathematics including algebra and pre-calculus. Any attempt to just leap into these fields of study without prior preparation will inevitably result in unnecessary frustration.

STAY POSITIVE

One of the most challenging obstacles you will face along your journey has nothing at all to do with your current skills, resources, or time. These challenges are manageable. The real obstacle is more about you—your own emotions and your thoughts.

Interestingly, the strength of human emotions is that they most often occur in direct proportion to the intensity of what you desire. The more you want something, the more emotional you tend to be about it.

In this case, if your vision for your own future is filled with high hopes and great aspirations, it is likely that your emotions will be equally intense. Fear of failure often accompanies visions of a grand and completely fulfilling future.

Fear of failure is magnified when you consider the possibility of not being able to create your vision and reach your desired goal. The real danger of derailment along the journey comes from the thoughts in your own head. Do the following thoughts sound familiar?

- What will people think if I fail?

- How will I get the money when I'm just making ends meet today?
- How will I find the time when I already feel stressed looking at my to-do list each day?
- What if I struggle and cannot handle the academic load?
- Am I smart enough to earn a college degree?

While no one can tell you what specific emotions you will experience, research confirms that returning to the classroom is a highly emotional experience for most adult learners. I remember my own emotional experiences when I took on the challenge of earning my degrees. Those were intensely emotional times. I was no different than you. I had self-doubt.

I asked myself: What am I doing in this class? Why does it seem that everyone else is so much smarter than I am? How am I going to get all this done? Where am I going to get the money I need to pay tuition? Why am I home studying when I could be out having fun?

When carefully managed, however, your emotions can also be an important sustaining element along the journey. Creating the vision of the future you desire for yourself, knowing that your efforts will improve possibilities for you and your loved ones, and taking the steps to realize that vision will produce positive emotions that can sustain you through difficult times.

No matter how challenging the task to earn your degree, no one will ever be able to take away your great accomplishment. The poet Joseph Addison said, "Education is a companion whom no misfortune can depress, no crime can destroy, no enemy can alienate, and no despotism can enslave."

When you combine the information obtained in the "to-be" process of visualizing your future with the "to-do" tasks of performing a self-assessment, the result is the important information you need about yourself to begin the journey. Your inventory will encompass your skills, your strengths, your weaknesses, your desires, and, above all, your vision of the future life you are creating for yourself. These are like the GPS coordinates that launch you in the right direction on your journey.

ACTION STEPS

- Create a journal with your vision of the future documented. Update it over time.
- Complete the self-assessment tool located in this book.
- Build an inventory of Internet sites that provide data and valuable information you can use along the journey.
- Take the Strong Interest Inventory at www.cpp.com and compare these answers to the personal interest profile you created in the self-inventory in this book.
- Reflect on your earlier education and career and what it would have meant to your life if you had had these resources available to you at the beginning of your journey.

■ ■ ■

04

YOU HAVE COMPETITION FOR THE CAREER YOU WANT

You are probably among almost 40 million Americans who have some college credit—but didn't finish their degrees. Yet over the past several decades, millions of adult learners have successfully completed their degrees. It is likely that they used one or more of the resources outlined in the chapters of this book.

They too encountered and addressed similar hurdles to those you now face. They overcame challenges. They conquered fears and anxieties about whether they were smart enough and could do the work. They found financial resources to pay for tuition while providing for their families. And many of them held full-time jobs and took classes too.

In the end, they were successful because they followed a road map to achieving their goals to earn their degrees. You need to have your own road map.

No matter what your hurdles are, this book provides that personal road map for you. I am sure many of those successful degree holders who have gone before you would encourage you to do the same.

THE SHEER NUMBERS

The majority of college enrollees today are considered nontraditional students. The National Center for Education Statistics (NCES) included anyone who satisfies at least one of the following as a nontraditional student:

- Delays enrollment. These are high school graduates who immediately go to work or enlist in active duty military service.

- Attends part-time for at least part of the academic year.

- Works full-time (thirty-five hours or more per week) while enrolled.

- Is considered financially independent for purposes of determining eligibility for financial aid.

- Has dependents other than a spouse (usually children, but sometimes others such as a parent or sibling).

- Is a single parent (either not married or married but separated and has dependents).

- Does not have a high school diploma (did not complete traditional high school but did complete nontraditional high school graduation requirements such as a GED or other high school completion certificate).

By this standard, the NCES determined that 73 percent of all undergraduates could be considered nontraditional, representing the newly "typical" undergraduate.

Many of these nontraditional students already have some or most of the credits required to graduate. Forty-five percent have completed one to two years of college; 25 percent have completed three to four years of college; and, surprisingly, another 25 percent report having completed over three-fourths of their degree requirements before deciding to take time off from school. They are on their way to earning a degree.

Now is a good time to think about where you are in the process. It is very likely that when you enroll in your college degree program you will meet one or more of these attributes and thus be a nontraditional student yourself.

LIFE IS DIFFERENT

As an adult learner, you are not the same person you were when you may have abandoned your college education the last time. Your life has probably changed dramatically since the first time you stepped foot onto a college campus perhaps as a young high school graduate.

YOU ARE NOT THE SAME PERSON YOU WERE WHEN YOU MAY HAVE ABANDONED YOUR COLLEGE EDUCATION THE LAST TIME.

Previously, you may have lived on campus and studied in a classroom. A professor gave classroom lectures. You took courses, classes, and final exams. You used textbooks and libraries. You wrote papers. You had a social life that included peers and a broader college community.

Studying was primary, while work supplemented the cost of education and your social life. You probably did not have children yet. Rather, your parents supported you emotionally and financially. You were part of a national culture that honors and celebrates "college for our kids."

But, today, your life is changed. You are not alone. The world has changed. And the college experience will be different for you.

In your first college experience, you had a structure for managing time. Classes were scheduled at a fixed time and in fixed places on the campus grounds. Your degree plan included a well-defined progression from your freshman to senior year. You had academic calendars with time off in the summer.

Perhaps even the process of selecting your major, enrolling in classes, and doing your homework was based on someone else's expectations—parents, siblings, high school teachers, guidance counselors, or professors. Your primary source of motivation likely was external to yourself. Let me explain.

Maybe your parents (or a teacher) told you that going to college was the right thing to do. You may even have been one of those students whose parents simply said, "You will go to college," and they backed up their wishes by paying all your expenses.

These are also likely to be parents who earned their own college degrees and know, as I do, that an education is critical in today's highly competitive world.

Interestingly, research shows that the number one predictor of degree attainment is whether a student's parents earned college degrees. If your mother or father graduated from college, in other words, chances are you will too.

THE NUMBER ONE PREDICTOR OF DEGREE ATTAINMENT IS WHETHER A STUDENT'S PARENTS EARNED COLLEGE DEGREES.

But even in the face of all this (pressure, expectations), you did not finish, and you are now in the position of having to seriously consider going back.

What is different this time? Everything is up to you—not your parents or a guidance counselor or a mentor.

As an adult returning to college, you must provide your own source of motivation along with the other resources you will need. Now you will be the one who takes responsibility for the decisions you make about your future.

One group of adult learners with special needs is represented by returning military personnel. For these veterans the decisions required can be even more challenging than for their civilian counterparts. Some veterans didn't have the opportunity or weren't ready to attend college directly out of high school.

Returning from active duty is difficult enough, but factor in the change in structure of military life to the college environment, and this transition can be truly overwhelming. Veterans exiting active duty are coming out of a highly structured environment into the extremely diverse setting of college life. For veterans, forming a powerful vision for their future is even more of a necessity.

With their mission-driven military training and experience, the successful veterans create a new civilian mission for themselves. By so doing they create the purpose needed to motivate and sustain themselves. A purposeful civilian life through the pursuit of an education is the new mission they most often define for themselves.

Some universities are better at serving these retired men and women in this critical repurposing in their lives. For you veterans, selecting the university that fits your needs is critical. Specific help for your understanding of how to translate military MOS to civilian careers and other active duty to civilian transition details are available in chapter 12: Especially for Veterans.

Successful adult learners balance a wide range of issues so common to life in this day and age. If you are to follow your successful path, you will need to strike a balance in your daily routine.

With little or no extra time left in the margins of your day, you will find increases in pressures that make attending class, focusing, and completing homework on time much more difficult. No matter what special circumstances you are facing, recognizing these obstacles and being sensitive to issues that led to leaving your studies in the first place can help you stay the course and complete your degree.

OVERCOMING FIRST-TIME OBSTACLES

Let's talk about why many college students left before completing their degrees. Here are the top reasons returning students mentioned, according to an accredited university research project.

- *Family obligations.* These can arise at any time, whether it is a new baby, illness, or a death in the family. Many adult students are sandwiched between parenting responsibilities and caring for aging parents—both requiring their attention and leaving no time for studies.

"I have started and stopped school twice; both times were because I had just recently had a child."

"My dad became ill, and I could not afford to pay someone to take care of him while I go to school. As a result, I had to put my education on hold for the time."

"My son was born early and with complications, so it was too hard to go back."

You may now be the parent, and your role as a parent can have a significant influence on the degree-seeking experience.

• *Juggling finances.* Balancing the growing expenses of being a student with the diminishing income from a reduced work schedule can make college an unaffordable option for many wanting to resume education. The Bill and Melinda Gates Foundation funded a study with the consulting firm Public Agenda called "With Their Whole Lives Ahead of Them." This study found the primary reason traditional campus-based students drop out is because they had to work more to support themselves.

Although the issue of finances affects many returning adult students, women seem to have fewer financial options and as a result rely more on loans to finance higher education. Women account for 72 percent of all returning students. Because more adult students are working adults who fund their own education, a job loss would be detrimental to degree attainment without other resources.

"The classes were more than I could afford at the time due to not having a full-time job anymore."

"I would really like to continue my degree since I am so close to completion; however, due to the cost of the courses and my current financial situation, things aren't going to work out for a while. A payment plan would be great, but I haven't seen anything about the university offering this option. Another thing is that I need only three more classes, but I live over seven hours away and all of the courses I have taken to date have been online. The final classes I need to complete my degree are not offered online. Could I take this elsewhere and transfer the credits? Is there any way to make exceptions and have the student work the material without being in attendance in class? Any help you could offer would be great."

The good news is that financial challenges can be overcome. In a recent study of over 900 Bellevue University graduates, 92 percent were working while studying for their degree. Of those surveyed, almost half had access to employee tuition assistance. Paying continuing-education tuition is a commonly offered employee benefit many companies use to attract and retain high-performance employees.

- *Lack of support.* The majority of *dormant students* (a term I use to refer to students who have taken some college but not been awarded their degree) interviewed did not feel that their college supported them adequately while they were enrolled. Most believed that their colleges did little or nothing to help them when they dropped out. Worse, once these former students no longer had regular contact with their former university, they became even more isolated over time. The sense of isolation not only involved a lack of support from schools, many dormant students pointed to a lack of support from employers and family. Finally, their isolation made it more difficult to develop that important relationship with a mentor. Ultimately, most dormant students dropped out not because they were dissatisfied with the coursework, but because they felt they had no other recourse. They simply did not feel they had the support they needed at school, at home, or at work.

"I felt lost and alone; very sad to have failed in something that should have been a positive time in my life."

"I was fearful of telling my supervisor and my coworkers that I was considering going back to school. Most of them don't even know that I don't have my degree."

"I hesitate to call a college because I am afraid that they'll put the hard sell on me and try to get me to enroll. I'm just not ready to pick a university yet."

"I was so depleted of strength and motivation. My feelings went from excited and energetic when I first started college, to depressed and overwhelmed by the time I decided to take a break."

If these comments reflect your feelings, take heart. Let this book be your personal guide and mentor to avoid a repeat performance as you re-enroll on your path to earning your degree.

THE ROLE OF THE UNIVERSITY

Universities have a limited ability to help adult learners address the obstacles of navigating family obligations and challenges at work. But in some ways this is changing. Some colleges and universities are reaching out to previously enrolled students and retaining them once they have re-enrolled. However more needs to be done.

Based on university research survey results, former dormant students who have since graduated suggested that schools could be doing much more to help returning students attain their degrees. For example, traditional campus-based universities could offer more opportunities and programs that allow for part-time study and offer more financial aid and childcare options. They could provide mentoring, nontraditional class times (evenings, weekends, and online courses). Efforts in these directions could significantly ease the way for returning students.

Perhaps you tried to work with your college before you dropped out, but you faced a seemingly insurmountable bureaucracy. Our research shows only 15 percent of dormant students said that their school took any action to help retain them. In many cases, the general sense was:

YOUR FUTURE IS CALLING

"They were in it for the money and could not care less. I was upset and discouraged."

You may have felt the same way and had mixed emotions about your decision to take time off. Maybe you took the only choice available to you at the time. As you reflect, you may regret your decision and wish you had been able to find a way to stay enrolled. Fortunately, you have a second chance.

FORTUNATELY, YOU HAVE A SECOND CHANCE.

EMOTIONAL STRENGTH

Whatever the reason for your leaving school, you can move past your former college experience and formulate the solution to complete your degree while balancing work, family, and social life. Yes, it will require a reallocation of your scarce financial resources and ever precious time. But your personal road map will keep you connected powerfully to the vision of your future. With commitment, you can do this! You can create a better future for yourself and your loved ones.

Stories from former dormant students may provide you with the confidence you need to succeed.

- One student said in the research, "I was finally stable with a place to live and a permanent job which gave me the security to take a risk like stealing all my free time for school. It was also the fact that my company was willing to pay for the degree program I had always wanted to pursue."

- Another individual reported, "I had very frank discussions with my boss about my career and how my lack of a degree meant I could not receive certain promotions regardless of how hard I worked or how well I did my job."

Degrees completed, former dormant students encourage others to seek out college counselors and advisors to discuss their goals and the obstacles to achieving them. If you reach out, these professionals are there to help you work out a plan. They will assess your personal financial situation and develop a combination of aid sources such as grants, scholarships, and loans that can ease your transition back to class. There is more about this in chapter 11: How to Pay for College.

Recent adult graduates recommend holding a family meeting to share your desires and goals for completing your education. This will lay the groundwork for getting support from your immediate family and enable others to see that this journey is in the best interest of the entire family. Support from your loved ones can be a monumental motivator! The end result benefits not only you but your family as well.

MENTORS AND GUIDES

Time and time again, we hear from adult learners who have graduated about the importance of having a trusted mentor. This is especially true when there are no degree holders in your immediate family. These mentors serve as an important source of information as well as being a critical source of motivation for you as a returning student. They can help you stay committed.

Who has the potential to be a mentor? A good friend, coworker, family member, minister, or counselor. Anyone who will support you in your desire to return to school can help. Mentors are especially important when you feel discouraged or encounter a lack of support from a boss or loved one. A mentor can help you plan your personal road map to your desired future.

With your personal vision, your road map, and a trusted mentor, you will find the solution that fits your needs in terms of convenience, time, and finances. Start by exploring your options and gathering advice from mentors you trust and respect. Your confidants will want to help you reach your goals, and at the same time, they can help calm your anxieties by providing objective guidance.

Gather information from potential educational institutions about what you need and what you can expect. Share this information with your mentor or mentors. Their wisdom can help you. While you do the work, their advice, wise counsel, and guidance create an environment of support so that you do not feel alone.

GRADUATION—BEING THERE

There's nothing quite like being there. Picture yourself at your graduation ceremony alongside other nontraditional students. Look around you. In the audience sit your proud family and friends. Diplomas are presented individually by faculty, deans, and officers of the university as you and fellow graduates walk triumphantly across the stage.

As each academic presenter looks into your eyes, they see your overflowing joy and pride. When your name is read aloud, loved ones in the audience erupt with applause and cheering. Some shout your name and applaud. What an achievement! In that moment, allow yourself to bask in the feeling of knowing you have accomplished this major task—knowing that you earned your degree. No one can ever take away your accomplishment. You earned it.

ACTION STEPS

- Ask at least three adults who are either enrolled in college today or have finished their degrees within the last two years to share their experiences.

- Have a conversation with your significant other or those people closest to you about your plans to earn your degree.

- Find at least two trusted mentors who can share their college experiences and support you and the decisions you make as you move forward.

■　■　■

05

FINISH YOUR DEGREE?
WHY BOTHER?

Here's the key question every individual who is considering a return to college needs to ask: "Why bother finishing that degree?" Your reasons might be very practical. You might be motivated to complete your degree because you want these concrete benefits:

- A better job
- Higher wages
- To be a more informed and better citizen
- A significantly increased likelihood that your children will get a college education
- Greater emotional health and lifelong satisfaction
- A new, more purposeful life

Research shows that these factors are important for a significant number of degree seekers. In addition, as you strive to succeed in today's economy, higher education becomes critically important. To succeed individually and as a nation, we all need to have a more educated workforce.

A recent survey by Georgetown University reports that by 2018, 63 percent of all new jobs in the U.S. will require workers who have at least some college education. This is especially important when so many are asking the question in today's marketplace: "Is a college degree really worth it?"

This book is all about the decisions you are making today to create your own desired future. The most important thing about that future is what the American economy will look like when you get your degree, not what the world looks like today.

THE MOST IMPORTANT THING ABOUT THAT FUTURE IS WHAT THE AMERICAN ECONOMY WILL LOOK LIKE WHEN YOU GET YOUR DEGREE, NOT WHAT THE WORLD LOOKS LIKE TODAY.

IS GETTING A DEGREE WORTH THE SACRIFICE?

"In every study that's been done, the results are black and white. College greatly enhances the earnings potential," said Duke University's Vivek Wadhwa, an educator, researcher, and entrepreneur. While not every person who earns a degree automatically has a great career, as we have already seen, the fact is that a college degree is, by far, the most important asset you can have to improve your chances for a more prosperous and secure future.

Anthony Carnevale, director of the Georgetown University Center on Education and the Workforce, estimates that *on average* a bachelor's degree is now worth about $1.2 million more than a high school diploma in lifetime earnings.

A BACHELOR'S DEGREE IS NOW WORTH ABOUT $1.2 MILLION MORE THAN A HIGH SCHOOL DIPLOMA IN LIFETIME EARNINGS.

But this is not just about getting a bachelor's degree. It is about your future. Virtually any post-secondary learning can boost income. A two-year associate of arts degree on average is worth about $425,000 more than a high school diploma in lifetime earning potential, and college dropouts still earn on average $240,000 more than students who stop at high school. The bottom line could not be clearer. Learning vastly improves the odds of advancing your career and increasing your income.

The benefits of earning a degree extend beyond you. For the graduate, the degree is symbolic of every hurdle overcome in order to make it through to graduation. It's about self-confidence and assurance that you are capable of accomplishing a challenging mission. The degree also symbolizes a green flashing light to proceed with advancing your career.

To your family a degree represents a higher standard of living and the potential for putting the family on the path to prosperity. It makes you a symbol to those around you that education is important. To our country, you are a citizen who can help society and compete in the global economy.

Completing a college degree, however, is not just about jobs, income, and status. There are deeper reasons that go to the core of who you are as a human being. Fundamentally, earning a college degree has the potential to transform your life in a profound and positive way. As a college graduate, you get the following additional benefits:

- Gain self-confidence
- Find out how to learn from others and recognize that knowledge is valuable
- Be equipped to understand complex issues
- Be able to communicate more effectively with those around you, including your loved ones
- Make sound decisions and know how to better deal with an uncertain future
- Get skills to gather information and analyze it
- Learn how to learn and therefore be ready to be engaged in our complex and rapidly changing world

A college degree builds and solidifies those skills that are central to the twenty-first-century global economy. Earning a degree allows you to get more from life and helps you become a better person.

You will be a different person at the end of your journey. I know I was.

A PERSONAL STORY

You may be wondering what qualifies me to address the fundamental value of a college degree. Here's my story. Education literally transformed my life from what it might otherwise have been.

I am the oldest of four children from a lower-middle-class family in which no one had more than a high school diploma. We lived in a rural farming community about thirty miles west of Philadelphia. Money was scarce. My mother passed away when I was fifteen years old. At a very early age I had many of the responsibilities of an adult. To keep our family together I willingly assumed many of the duties of a parent. To earn the money to go to college, I worked outside the home mowing lawns, caddying at the local country club, and working as a day laborer on concrete and pipeline construction jobs.

My dad did not complete the eighth grade and only vaguely understood the importance of a college education. However, he supported my decision to go to college, believing it could improve my life. Like most parents he wanted a better life for his children.

Fortunately I had mentors outside of my family. My high school teachers encouraged me to pursue further education. In addition, my high school sweetheart came from a well-educated family, and both of her parents had college degrees. Because of their familiarity with the college application process, they became mentors for me when it was time to apply to college, and for that I was most grateful.

As a college student, I felt ill prepared for the academic work. At Carnegie Mellon University my classmates seemed far more prepared. I felt challenged to catch up. My dad encouraged me to continue and see the value inherent in my studies. Finances continued to be very tight, and I worked the entire time I was in college, both during the school year and during the breaks. I could not afford to own a car until after graduation.

A whole new world opened up for me in college. There wasn't much cultural diversity where I grew up. At Carnegie

Mellon University, however, there were international students. I suddenly saw how diverse the world is, and I was able to learn from those with different backgrounds. I began to participate in activities that encouraged critical thinking. I engaged in problem solving and in discussions about ideas. My world was expanding and I was learning. Life was good.

I developed other important skills in college, including the scientific discipline of experimentation, logical constructs, and creating hypotheses. I learned the importance of gathering and weighing evidence and objectively drawing inferences from data. These are skill sets just not available outside the higher education environment.

Additionally, I learned to appreciate new perspectives. I discovered that it's important to learn from others as well as figure things out on your own. I developed better oral and written communication skills. I was growing and changing. It was clear I was on a fulfilling path.

Finishing my bachelor's degree afforded me many personal and professional opportunities. Education opened lots of doors for me while expanding my vision of what was possible. I worked on challenging, interesting projects with talented colleagues and traveled the world.

I was so convinced of the importance of education that I decided to continue with graduate work, earning an MBA from the University of Pittsburgh and a Ph.D. from the University of California, Berkeley.

EDUCATION: THE GREAT DIFFERENTIATOR

Education paves the way to career development. Eighty percent of the people in the Bellevue University research study stated that getting a career was their motivation for completing their education. If you do the work recommended in this book, it will equip you with the information to select a career using the critical twenty-first-century skills that employers need and expect.

An education significantly increases your lifetime earnings and cuts in half your probability of being unemployed. It also makes you a more informed citizen, a better parent, and a better leader. Further, it improves your problem solving and communication skills. An education creates value for you as an individual, for the organization that employs you, and for your community, your children, and our nation.

THINK AND THINK AGAIN

Many of you have asked this question: "Is it really worth it to continue my education with all of the obstacles and challenges I will face along the way?" I know you're considering the question because you are reading this book.

Your life circumstances have positioned you to set out on the road to earn a college degree. Tens of millions have embarked upon this road, but many were detoured off their path. This time, your own experiences and your hopes for the future have led you back to the college path once again. Today, you are closer than ever to your personal goal of a college degree.

I hope my story and this book will provide you with the motivation you need to take the leap and make your college degree a reality. The bottom line is that, by completing my degree, I learned to live life with purpose. Quite simply, getting that degree makes all the difference in fulfilling your potential and being a better person. Why would you ever need a more compelling purpose for your journey?

ACTION STEPS

- Write down your personal reasons for wanting to earn a degree. Post these where you will see them often (on your bathroom mirror or the refrigerator).

- In your journal, write down three areas of your life you expect to improve once you earn your degree.

- What are three things about you that you feel represent unfulfilled potential? Write in your journal how the journey to getting this degree can help you fulfill this potential.

- With whom do you think it is important to share your experiences while earning your degree? With whom will you celebrate when you earn your degree? Who will be sitting in the audience as you walk across the stage and accept your degree? Write these names down and communicate your struggles and successes to them on this journey.

■   ■   ■

06

YOU CAN DO THIS

'm going to reveal a dirty little secret about higher education, but first, let's look at what's been happening in the world today.

It's almost passé to point out how much the world has changed in recent years. We no longer buy albums or CDs to listen to music. Instead, we purchase songs from iTunes that are downloaded onto our computers, iPods, or iPads. We get news through RSS feeds, from the Internet, or from our Facebook friends rather than from the evening network news.

And now for the dirty little secret: Higher education has not kept up with the pace of change. Designed for a different era, most traditional educational institutions do not serve the current needs of adults who are returning to college to finish their degrees. You'll want to reread that sentence, because it is true and that's why this book can help you navigate the ivy-covered walls, whether those walls are real or virtual.

Thirty years ago the majority of college students were recent high school graduates. Their number one priority was education. Maybe you were one of them. They didn't have to worry about mortgages, putting food on the table, attending their kids' soccer games, or losing their jobs.

As we have seen, many students pursuing higher education degrees now are nontraditional students, like you. These are students who are financially independent, attend part-time, have delayed enrollment, work or have worked full-time, have dependents, and may be parents. They have jobs and responsibilities as family breadwinners. They are just like you.

TRADITIONAL COLLEGES AND UNIVERSITIES

In light of these changes, why do traditional higher education institutions fail to meet the needs of nontraditional students? Consider this perspective. Institutions of higher education originally were designed to teach students "the wisdom of the ages."

TRADITIONAL HIGHER EDUCATION INSTITUTIONS FAIL TO MEET THE NEEDS OF NONTRADITIONAL STUDENTS.

Over the centuries humans put their capabilities of reasoning and communication to work to improve life for themselves and their communities. They examined the world around them and thought carefully about what they observed. They debated long and hard with their colleagues, designed experiments, and evaluated data.

This assembled body of knowledge led to the creation of the university where "wisdom of the ages" was archived and distributed in the millions of volumes of books and articles in publications stored in libraries and in scholarly lectures. Additionally, professors imparted this knowledge to students. Students attended classes on campus and learned on the schedule and timetable dictated by the needs of the institutions.

Contemporary traditional universities served a distinct mission: to socialize students entering adulthood on the ways of the world. Instead of tossing our children out of the safe confines of the family and directly into the larger society, the college campus provided a halfway house—a place to live away from home, join new communities (including fraternities and sororities), and associate with others with diverse backgrounds all while absorbing the wisdom of the ages. It was a place designed to learn how to be a productive adult contributing to society.

SHIFT GEARS

While traditional colleges and universities did a good job of educating and socializing young students for many years, they have been slow to adapt to a changing world outside of the campus. With structured class times, "brick and mortar" campuses have become less significant, especially for today's adult learners. Adult learners lead more complex lives and have more responsibilities than did the traditional student of the earlier era.

"BRICK AND MORTAR" CAMPUSES HAVE BECOME LESS SIGNIFICANT, ESPECIALLY FOR TODAY'S ADULT LEARNERS.

Today's nontraditional students are able to manage their lives with smart devices and Internet connectivity and therefore have much greater flexibility pursuing their higher education goals. To accomplish these goals they need colleges and universities to embrace a new model of providing quality education in a supportive, innovative, and less restrictive delivery mode. At the same time, adult learners need to recognize the unique obstacles they face as they return to pursue degrees and be ready to overcome them.

COMMON OBSTACLES TO RETURNING TO COLLEGE

As with almost anything in life, you will face obstacles in securing the vision of your future. These include many bumps in the road to finishing your college degree. Some obstacles will be small, such as worrying that most students in your classes will be younger and smarter than you. They probably won't be! In fact, the average college student is getting older every year.

Other challenges will be more difficult to overcome, such as finding the money and time to return to school. The information in this book helps you create a plan to overcome these obstacles. Let's look at them one by one.

• *Understanding the importance of investing in you.* Some dormant students don't see finishing their college education as an investment in themselves. They may not have the money to return to school and don't want to take on debt to pay for the completion of their degree. Or they don't want to be distracted from their current careers while finishing their education. Others are in a caregiver role with babies, aging parents, or others. Caregivers don't drop these responsibilities to go back to school, nor should they.

Many find the way to balance the needs of their loved ones with their priority to complete their degree. They do it by carving out a life balance between the demands of daily caregiving and learning. In the end, it is their powerful vision of the future that they have set out to create for themselves and the loved ones they are caring for that motivates them. It is the passion for the future that gives them the internal energy at the end of a long day to sit down and do the work to complete their learning and secure their degree. This energy comes from inside and sustains caregivers. They know that this is a journey that must be taken one step at a time, one course at a time.

- *Convenience.* Many dormant students cite lack of convenience as a reason for not completing their education. Their first college choice may be too far away or the classes are offered at times that make it impossible for the returning student to attend.

There are easy solutions to this obstacle. Many times a community college is located nearby and usually offers more convenient class times (with evening and weekend choices for those working during the day). There are a large number of online universities (both nonprofit and for-profit) that allow students to attend classes at their convenience. Resources for locating colleges and universities will be discussed in chapter 9: How to Pick the Right School.

- *Abundance of negative self-talk.* One of the hardest obstacles to overcome is the negative self-talk in which many dormant students engage. This self-imposed obstacle leaves many doubting their ability to finish their degree.

A student may be in a demanding job and doesn't know how to carve out time to go back to school. Or perhaps the student is struggling with competence and self-confidence issues. It's easy for dormant students to rationalize that they dropped out one (two or three) times before, and they have convinced themselves that they'll probably do it again. The self-imposed conclusion is they shouldn't bother giving college another try.

This lack of confidence in solving the problem creates a false belief that there is absolutely no way they ever can finish their degree.

If you are facing this obstacle, it's time to ask yourself, *How compelling is my vision of a better future for myself and my loved ones? Am I motivated to make the required adjustments in my life that I will have to make to actually secure this vision of my future?* If you want it badly enough, you will persevere despite life's curveballs and will succeed in reaching the end of the journey where your diploma awaits.

• *Addressing quality issues.* The perception of quality creates another obstacle shared by the majority of dormant students. They ask: "Is this a quality school?"

In a higher education program there are two widely held perceptions of quality. The first is selectivity. It is commonly assumed that schools that reject lots of applicants are higher quality. Not so. Selectivity only describes the quality of the students who attend that particular institution and by itself says little about the quality of the education provided by the institution itself. A better alternative, especially for nontraditional students, is to seek out other quality indicators.

The much-touted *US News and World Report* rankings only examine certain specific factors in preparing their annual list. The criteria have little to do with what a returning student might want to know to decide to finish a degree later in life. *US News and World Report* recently expanded its rankings to include online universities. Rather than concentrating on gaining admittance to an institution based on selectivity, focus on the quality of the institution's curriculum, the quality of the learning, and its affordability.

FOCUS ON THE QUALITY OF THE INSTITUTION'S CURRICULUM, THE QUALITY OF THE LEARNING, AND ITS AFFORDABILITY.

A second perception of quality relates to price. People tend to believe that high tuition means high quality. High price does not assure quality, and today there are many high-quality universities that do not have the highest prices.

There is one other important fact you need to know about the tuition costs posted on university websites. The fact is that many students who actually enroll do not pay these tuition costs. For more detail on what is happening at every accredited college and university in America, see the facts in chapter 9: How to Pick the Right School.

Additionally, it's possible to go to an expensive school and receive what others perceive as a "quality" education but end up with an education that does not fit who you are. It's also possible to go to less expensive and lesser-known institution and get both a terrific classroom (and social) experience and a quality education.

The challenge for you is to find high-quality education without the high price. You can achieve this by researching, locating, and evaluating objective data about each institution. There will be more on this in chapter 9: How to Pick the Right School.

• *Cost considerations.* Higher education has become very expensive in the United States.

As an adult student, you most likely will be paying for your own education. Your first priority is to reduce the total cost of your education. The high price/quality link actually works against your self-interest in this decision.

Then you need to look for ways to finance the cost. There are many ways to reduce the total cost of your education. It's important to find colleges and universities where you can get the most value for the assets you already have. Once you have selected the university that best fits you and your vision of your future, there are multiple sources of financing. It is more crucial than ever to identify and use all sources of funds as tuition continues to rise.

While it is possible to reduce costs considerably, it takes a focused effort and good, reliable data. More specifics about finding resources for returning to school will be covered in chapter 11: How to Pay for College.

There are other cost considerations besides tuition. When deciding where to apply or enroll, figure these costs into the equation:

• Books and other supplies

• Childcare fees if you have younger children

• Gas and parking fees

Additionally, think about the time involved in continuing your education in the cost equation. Many dormant students have additional factors in their lives, especially when compared to the typical eighteen-year-old student. As you know, some of these factors include families, careers, and professional and community and volunteer endeavors. All of these responsibilities take time.

Add to this the time involved in class, travel time to and from campus, the time involved in studying and working on assignments, the time involved in meeting with other students for group projects and study sessions, and, if you are missing work to attend school, the time needed to make up those hours. This time issue is a significant one to be aware of when assessing education choices. In evaluating what's doable, make sure that the institution's program fits with your schedule and your needs.

FIVE STEPS TO OVERCOME THE OBSTACLES

Throughout this book I have told you that you can succeed at finishing your college degree. Depending on your circumstances, it may not be easy. This journey, like any other, requires hard work, planning, and motivation to begin and complete. My goal is to make it a little easier and less stressful for you. As you continue on your journey, take these five steps to help overcome the obstacles:

1. *What are your current capabilities and resources?* Any good decision maker realizes the first step in planning a project is to measure the current status of available resources. In the same way, assessing your skills allows you to create a thorough plan for fulfilling your vision of the education journey. Determine if you have the basic skills for returning to school, such as the ability to use the software necessary

for completing assignments such as Microsoft Word. If not, create a plan to acquire these skills.

Also, there are other resources you will need to access to return to school. This is more than just having the money to pay for tuition. It includes items such as reliable transportation, a computer and Internet connection (or access to these perhaps at work with permission or at the library), and available time for attending classes, studying, group projects, and finishing assignments.

2. *What is your final education destination (educational institution, major)?* A major is more than what you will study while in college. It is an investment in what you are going to do for the rest of your life. The other critical decision is the institution you are going to choose. Which college or university offers your major, is affordable, and fits your schedule? More details on these decisions in chapter 7: How to Pick the Right Career for You and chapter 8: Where the Jobs Are - Today and Tomorrow—O*NET.

3. *What is your action plan for detours?* Oh, you will have diversions in your quest to finish your degree. Count on it. Planning for these before they happen will reduce your stress and make the trip less difficult. For example, determine who you will call if the babysitter cancels. Get contact information for other students in your classes so you can borrow their notes when you miss class due to business travel or other reasons. What if your car breaks down? Where will you go if your Internet isn't working and you need to submit an assignment? Write down every possible detour and think of a solution for each.

4. *Who is on your support team?* Ask friends and family from a variety of backgrounds to help as needed. Your team can

advise you as you face new obstacles along the way, especially when you hit those detours and unforeseen setbacks.

5. *What is the next step if you are continuing your education past a bachelor's degree?* With careful planning you can identify which courses are needed to finish your degree. However, if you plan on seeking a master's or a doctorate, explore the requirements for this continued course of study. There may be some classes you can take during your undergraduate studies. This simple step may save you time, money, and frustration.

THE DRIVE TO FINISH

Education provides you with the knowledge you need to be successful in this rapidly changing world we all live in today. It equips you to handle the complexities of today's world and determine what parts of the exploding quantity of information is most important for you and your career. But all the knowledge in the world will not help you finish your degree if you are lacking one crucial element: the motivation to finish.

Others can help motivate you, but it is your internal drive that you will come to depend upon. You have to want it enough to endure through the obstacles. Your vision of your future has to inspire and energize you every day of your journey. This is why it is important to have a powerful vision of your future that inspires you and fits "who you are."

In his book *The 7 Habits of Highly Effective People*, Stephen Covey said, "Start with the end in mind." The key is being resourceful and creative along the journey to finishing your degree. Constantly remind yourself of the reasons you made this decision to go back to college. Put up visual reminders of what this degree means to you. Post notes on your mirror. Be your own cheerleader and applaud yourself all the way to the end of this journey. When you make the decision to go back to college, you become the CEO of completing your degree. Don't let anything or anyone divert you from that path.

ACTION STEPS

- What are the two biggest obstacles to earning your degree? Document the necessary steps to overcome these obstacles. Refer to your personal reasons for earning a degree when obstacles seem insurmountable.
- Pick the three things that were most important to you when you went to college the *last time*. Write them down.
- Pick three things that are most important to you when you go back to school *this time*. Write them down. Compare them to your answers in the previous action step.
- If the traditional measures of education quality were price (high) and selectivity, what are your two most important quality measures now in selecting an institution?

■   ■   ■

07

HOW TO PICK THE RIGHT CAREER FOR YOU

I n our rapidly changing world, the old way no longer works. The traditional progression for high school graduates who embark on the college experience looks like this:

UNIVERSITY → MAJOR 1 → MAJOR 2 → MAJOR 3 → DEGREE → LOOK FOR A JOB → HOPE IT FITS WHO YOU ARE

Meaning: Get a job that fits your degree and hope that the job you find fits who you are

In this sequence, the fit between degree, job and who you are is the last thing in the sequence. This is the reason that so many people are unhappy with what they do with their lives every day.

In this sequence, the first decision high school seniors generally make is the selection of the college they plan to attend. This choice is based on several criteria, including geography, an alum in the family, the football team, brand reputation, and/or affordability. Then, after enrolling in the chosen college or university, students take general education courses in their freshman and sophomore years.

When students get to the junior year, they have to select a major for their degree. Although this decision is made in the present, it is really very much about the future. The major is the body of knowledge the student will use to make a living after graduating from college. The major is the body of knowledge the employer will be interested in once the student gets a degree. Think of the major as the answer to the employer's question: "What do you know and how will that be valuable to our company?"

WHAT DO YOU KNOW AND HOW WILL THAT BE VALUABLE TO OUR COMPANY?

Unfortunately, while professors are true experts in their subjects, they are ill equipped to advise students on what major to study. Professors are smart. They live within academic institutions where they interact with other professors every day. They can help the student learn the subject matter once the student has decided what he or she wants to learn. But professors have little ongoing involvement with the organizations that have the jobs college graduates are seeking. It is the managers of those hiring organizations, not the professors, who make the hiring decisions.

It is common for students to select a major course of study, and then a different major, and even sometimes switch to a new third major. Often there is little help from the experts, the professors, on what major to study. As we will see, the selection of a major should be based on who you are combined with the outlook for specific careers in the future. As smart as they are, professors are ill equipped to be good mentors on these issues.

These decisions about what to study are influenced largely by campus factors and experiences such as the difficulty experienced with certain courses. Circumstances in the external world and the rapid changes in the global economy usually are overlooked. Today, most graduates look for a job that fits their degree. Since there is often little planning about how the career fits, many graduates experience real challenges in just finding a job, let alone a career that fits "who they are."

As an adult learner, it is time for you to rethink how to make the critical decisions that will lead you to complete your college degree. If you followed the traditional path—selecting a university and then changing your major a few times—your current college transcript probably shows a lot of credits but no degree.

Your degree path looked like this:

UNIVERSITY → MAJOR 1 → MAJOR 2 → MAJOR 3 → DEGREE → LOOK FOR A JOB →

Only you found yourself stuck after investing in lots of classes without finishing a degree. To avoid a repeat performance, it's important to understand the differences between your first college experience and the opportunities ahead of you now.

First, you might not be interested in the same field of study. Since your first college experience, you probably have been exposed to a variety of life and work experiences. These may have sparked your interest in subjects more related to your strengths and passions than what you originally studied in college.

LIFE AND WORK EXPERIENCES MAY HAVE SPARKED YOUR INTEREST IN SUBJECTS MORE RELATED TO YOUR STRENGTHS AND PASSIONS THAN WHAT YOU ORIGINALLY STUDIED IN COLLEGE.

Second, recognize that the traditional higher education system is designed primarily to serve recent high school graduates. The traditional system presumes entering freshmen are going to stay on campus for four years and complete their degrees. Over those four years educational institutions give their students maximum flexibility to pick what to study and the space they need to find themselves. This approach is designed to help our young figure out who they are and what they want to do with their lives. At that stage of life, our young have the time they need to do this.

In your case, time is not your friend. You have a life and obligations. When you were young, you may have had the time and the use of money from your parents. Today it is highly likely you have limited time and money. "Figuring it out" while you attend classes is not an attractive option. You need to get on the right path from the beginning and then be efficient with every step you take.

The decisions you have to make now are not about whether to go to the university football game or who you are going to ask to the sorority party. The decision you have to make now is about the rest of your life. The rest of your life is competing for the resources that you need to make that future life happen. Today you need a much more effective approach to completing your degree. Today your decision should look like this:

WHO YOU ARE → CAREER → MAJOR → UNIVERSITY → DEGREE → FIND THE JOB THAT FITS WHO YOU ARE

With this approach you get to the job that fits you because that is where you began your decision process, not where you ended it. Unfortunately, adult learners receive little or no guidance on how to navigate these choices. As we have already seen, even within the university setting, many faculty members who are experts in their own disciplines are not well-informed about today's job market.

Fortunately, there are excellent outside resources to help you make these important decisions. One of them—O*NET from the U.S. Department of Labor—is described in detail in chapter 8: Where the Jobs Are - Today and Tomorrow—O*NET. Although your first inclination may be to skip over the pre-decision effort recommended in this chapter, I caution against that. Often it is only after you get into trouble and find out that you selected the wrong major that you take the steps to figure out the right one.

It is important that you not select the next major solely because you did not like the last one you picked (something you found out only after considerable effort invested). That's why it is essential for you as an adult learner to conduct the research and invest in the effort *before* selecting a major, a career, and finally a university. The effort invested in making these choices is critical for laying the foundation for a happy and prosperous career and avoiding the mistakes you may have made before.

THE CHALLENGES IN CHOOSING A FIELD OF STUDY

What do you want to be when you grow up? Surprise! That day has arrived. It is time to stop dreaming and start doing.

Unlike traditional college students, many adult learners (including veterans) have a current career or significant experience in industry. Therefore, the first decision that you face is whether to stay in your current industry or obtain a degree in something different in order to seek new career opportunities.

If you decide to stay in your current field, research industry-specific growth opportunities to decide on the most appropriate field of study within that industry. For example, you may enjoy your position in the computer industry and automatically assume that a computer science degree is what you need to advance in the field. However, there are a variety of other computer-related careers, such as Information Systems Manager or Web Developer, and other degrees such as Computer Networking, Health Information Management, and Web Design and Development to consider and explore.

If you make the decision to change your career, the first step is to take an objective self-assessment to determine who you are and what your strengths and passions are.

Select a career that fits your personality, strengths, and interests. Match what makes you successful in your chosen field and who you are as a person. Education can help you develop new skills and the knowledge needed to make the most of your talents and experience. Education can enhance your potential, but education cannot fundamentally change who you are, what you are good at, and how you deal with new situations.

That's why, if you look at careers and make a selection based on high salaries or prestige and status, or external influencers (what your spouse or coworkers say you should be), the result could be completing a degree for a career that you do not enjoy or find fulfilling.

One of the most compelling pieces of evidence about the mismatch between majors and careers are the large number of college graduates who are having difficulty finding jobs in today's job market. There are over 4.5 million unfilled jobs and in 2014 there were over 56 million positions filled with new hires. This is why it's crucial to research careers that satisfy both your strengths and the actual demands of the job market.

Your degree is your bridge between who you are and what the external market needs. If you choose poorly, you may end up with an expensive piece of paper and no job to help you pay for it. This is one reason there is so much talk today about "is a college degree worth it?" The reason some have a degree and no job is because the degree they have is not what the market needs in the way of skills and education.

YOUR DEGREE IS YOUR BRIDGE BETWEEN WHO YOU ARE AND WHAT THE EXTERNAL MARKET NEEDS.

Hiring managers are harshly objective. They do not care who you are. They care about what you can do. You have to do the *who you are* part. You do this by making sure that what you can do (your degree) matches who you are and that it also matches what employers are looking for.

In the end, the sad truth is that merely having a degree is not enough. The harsh reality is that when you make bad decisions in the beginning of this journey, you are likely to end up with a degree, all of the debt, and no job. When that happens, the answer to the real question, "Is *your* degree worth it?" is no. This is precisely why the work in this book is so important to your future.

PERSONAL ASSESSMENTS

Did you ever take one of those self-assessments in a popular women's magazine or online? Like "Are you a good lover?" or "What would you do in this situation?" And then the answers are given: "If you answered (c) to most questions, then you blah blah blah." Those are just games, but we like them because you and I like to measure ourselves against others.

Those magazine surveys have no scientific merit. They merely make you feel good. But many self-assessments can be excellent predictors of your personal attributes and career aspirations. Why don't you take one? They have the potential to reveal a field of study you hadn't even thought about, such as artistic individuals working in the accounting industry or outgoing people going into teaching.

Here are two suggested assessments to impartially help you determine a career based on your strengths and passions:

• *Gallup SF-34*. This instrument is available with the purchase of the book *StrengthsFinder 2.0* by Tom Rath. Do not buy a used copy because it contains an access code that can only be used once. The assessment is completed online with information from the book used to discover and understand your top five talents.

- *Myers-Briggs Type Indicator.* This instrument is
available online.
http://ficws.com/MBTI This assessment provides feedback
on four important dimensions of your personality:

    - **Favorite world:** Do you prefer to focus on the
    outer world or on your own inner world?

    - **Information:** Do you prefer to focus on the basic
    information you take in or do you prefer to
    interpret and add meaning?

    - **Decisions:** When making decisions, do you
    prefer to first look at logic and consistency or first
    look at the people and special circumstances?

    - **Structure:** In dealing with the outside world, do
    you prefer to get things decided or do you prefer
    to stay open to new information and options?

Notice that these attributes are very much about *who you
are*, which is exactly where you need to begin this decision.

Once you have a thorough understanding of who you are
and your strengths and passions, it's time to move on to the
next step—researching potential careers.

ACTION STEPS

- Review your self-inventory at the end of the book.

- Reflect on how you picked the university (universities)
that you attended in the past. If you attended more than
one, write down how the reason for your choices
changed between the first and the last.

- When you selected your major(s) before, what data about careers did you look at before you made the choice or choices?

- How well does the work you are doing in your job today fit "who you are"? What would you change?

- What are you really passionate about? What stops you from doing exactly what you are passionate about every working day of your life?

■　■　■

08

WHERE THE JOBS ARE – TODAY AND TOMORROW – O*NET

Here is where you actually get to try on the career (just as if you were trying on a pair of shoes) to see what fits you. If you've done the self-assessment work so far through the chapters, you're ready to move on because you now have a good idea about who you are. It's time to start trying careers on for fit.

I hope, by this point, it has become obvious why it is so important that you don't just take the tips I gave you earlier. In the end, only you can determine who you are. And only you can experience the career choices for the fit with what you want to do with the rest of your life.

You may want to select a career that gives you the potential for maximum income. Or on the other hand, money may not be that important to you and instead you want to do what would satisfy you in say a green career. Yet again, you may want to do public service where the pay is often much lower than in the private sector. Or you might want to work for a nonprofit.

You have to do the work. In the end, no one else can do this for you. No one else can tell what fits you.

The important thing is that only you can decide what is really valuable to you as you respond to the urge that your future is calling. Notice that this is not about my future, nor is it about the future of someone else.

Now it's time to take the information you discovered in your self-assessment and explore it further. This chapter will help you first select a career, then select a college major.

This step will guide you through O*NET, a website created under the sponsorship of the U.S. Department of Labor which has been developed by a consortium of human resource professionals. This site contains an enormous amount of valuable information on nearly 1,000 individual careers in the U.S. economy. It is a terrific resource to help you make decisions and is explored extensively throughout this chapter.

To get the most out of O*NET, assess your personal circumstances and think of yourself as being in one of the four following situations in your decisions:

1. You believe you know EXACTLY which career is right for you.

2. You don't know what career you want but you do know that you want to be in a particular industry.

3. You don't have a clue about what you want to do.

4. You are a veteran.

Together, we will explore all four situations in detail.

To get ideas about how best to use O*NET, let's examine information from O*NET for three different careers selected at random. The important thing to consider is how well these careers do or do not fit who you are. Remember, there are a total of nearly 1,000 careers on O*NET. These are just three examples.

Computer and Information Systems Manager. Someone in this position would review project plans and coordinate project activity; manage the back-up, security, and user help systems; and develop and interpret organizational goals, policies, and procedures. People in this career would be dependable, have integrity, be adaptable, pay attention to detail, foster cooperation among team members, and have analytical thinking skills. This occupation had a median salary in 2012 of $120,950 annually, and the demand for this position is growing. A bachelor's or master's degree is generally required.

Marriage and Family Therapist. Someone in this job would ask questions to help clients identify their feelings and behaviors; counsel clients on concerns, such as unsatisfactory relationships, divorce and separation, child rearing, home management, and financial difficulties; and encourage individuals and family members to develop and use skills and strategies for confronting their problems in a constructive manner. Such a therapist would be dependable, have integrity, show self-control, be able to handle stress, be cooperative, and have concern for others. The median salary in 2012 of $46,670 annually, and a master's or doctoral/professional degree is needed.

Graphic Designer. Someone in this position would create designs, concepts, and sample layouts based on knowledge of layout principles and esthetic design concepts, determine size and arrangements of illustrative material and copy, and select style and size of type after talking with clients to discuss and determine layout design. A graphic designer would be dependable and adaptable, show initiative, be able to handle stress, and be innovative with attention to detail. The median salary in 2012 of $44,150 annually, and a bachelor's or an associate's degree is required.

Let's look at these three quite different careers and draw some conclusions. If you want to interact with people and make a direct contribution to others, you probably will not want to study to be a Computer and Information Systems Manager, even though the salary is very attractive. Working with highly structured computer systems requires doing logical work and analyses, and you will often have to work alone. If you are not good at math or do not enjoy math, this career would make you miserable. Or, if you are creative and artistic, you may not want to become a Therapist and listen to relationship problems day after day.

But if you have a creative flair, you might consider Graphic Design. On the other hand, if you're the person everyone turns to for advice, and you enjoy helping others, becoming a Therapist may be for you.

If you are ready to begin the selection of your major, go to O*NET http://ficws.com/ONET and examine each career you are considering. Then you can narrow the alternatives based on your personality and your desired future and the steps required to achieve the goal. The major categories for each career are knowledge, skills, abilities, and technology.

• *Knowledge.* This category involves what you need to know. For example, the knowledge needed to be an accountant includes understanding a large number of detailed accounting principles, economics, math, including algebra and statistics, English language, and computer software.

- *Skills.* This category includes basic abilities and problem solving. To be an accountant, your skills need to include listening to others without interrupting and asking good questions. Accountants also must use math to solve problems. Finally, accountants must be skilled at thinking about the pros and cons of different options and picking the best one from among many. Today accountants work almost exclusively on computer systems using complex and sophisticated computer software to enter and analyze large bodies of data. A demonstrated skill in using that software is required to be an accountant.

- *Abilities.* Abilities refers to aptitudes in categories such as math, verbal, and communication skills. For example, accountants must have the ability to choose the right math to solve a problem. They must have the attention span to listen intently to what others say and to be able to read and understand what others have written. They need to come up with answers to lots of information. Finally, accountants must be able to pay close attention to details without being distracted.

- *Technology.* This category covers software and computer programs that might be used in the career you are considering. Knowing what technology a career uses allows you to explore these programs and is an additional dimension to selecting a career.

Other elements in making a career choice include, first and foremost, the outlook for that career. Will jobs in that field be available in the future, when you have finished your degree? O*NET has identified specific industries with what they call "a bright future" [go to Find Occupations and choose Bright Outlook from the dropdown box]. For each of the nearly 1,000 careers, the site shows whether that particular career has a bright future. To be considered a bright future, a career must meet one or more of the following criteria:

- Will grow rapidly in the next few years
- Will have a large number of openings
- Represents new and emerging occupations

O*NET shows all of the careers that have bright futures, and you should examine all the careers with Bright Outlook sometime in your search.
http://ficws.com/Occupations-Outlook

Obviously careers you are considering with a bright future are probably more attractive to you than careers that have a declining future. O*NET always identifies specific careers that have a bright future.

Finally, consider whether the industry you are considering is really of importance to you. You may already be in an industry that you know and have experience in, or you may be working for a company in an industry and you want to build on that experience to advance your career with your current employer. These data, by industry, are also available on O*NET by navigating from the home page to the Find Occupations dropdown box and selecting Industry.
http://ficws.com/Careers-Industry

HOW TO USE O*NET

The good news about O*NET is that there is a vast warehouse full of valuable information presented many different ways. The bad news is that it can be overwhelming and challenging to navigate. Plan to spend a month and take time to evaluate the near infinite number of choices on the website. Your investment of time is well worth your effort. The way to think about that effort is to view it as an investment—an investment in matching career choices and majors to *future* job opportunities and who you are.

If you do not make the investment in time and energy at this point, you will wind up investing even more time and energy trying to find a job that fits your degree. Not doing the work here increases the likelihood that you will be one of those with a degree, lots of debt, and no job to show for it.

To begin, use your Internet browser to go to O*NET. http://ficws.com/ONET Log on. It is important to note that here in the book I show only the top of the page. In many cases there is more information lower in the window. To see the full information you will need to click inside the window and use the down arrow on your keyboard or mouse to scroll the entire content.

When you log on, this is what you will see:

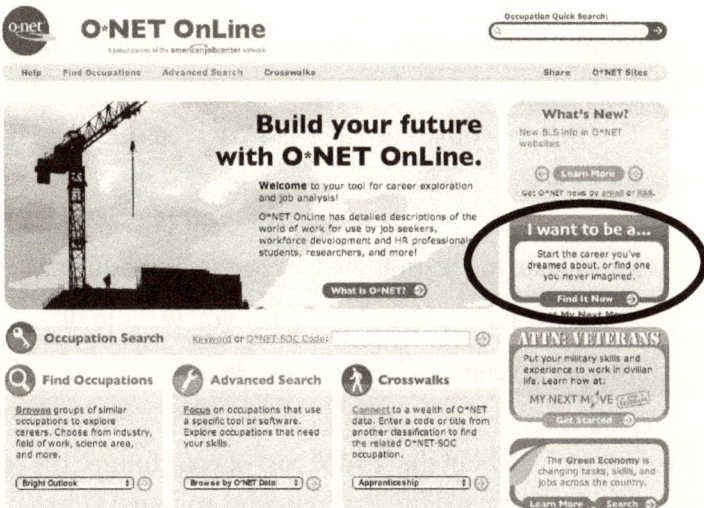

From here you have options. Under the block on the right I want to be a... you will be able to build your search based on who you are. Click on: Find it Now in the block, and this is what you will see:

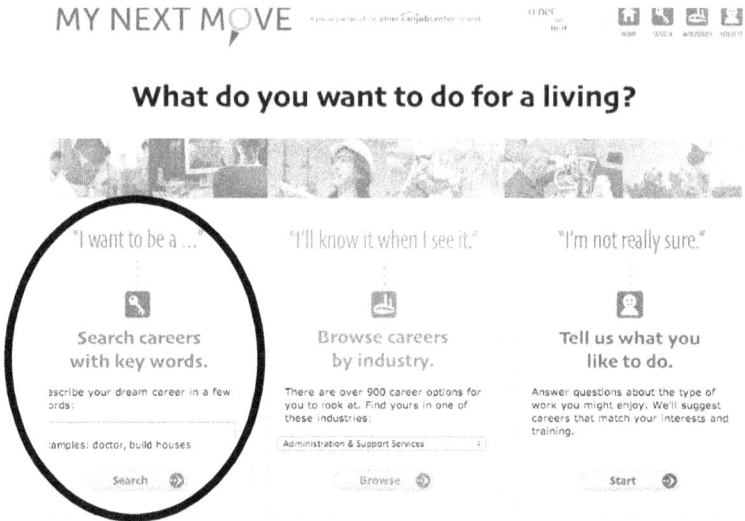

MY NEXT MOVE

What do you want to do for a living?

"I want to be a ..."

Search careers
with key words.

escribe your dream career in a few
ords:

:amples: doctor, build houses

Search

"I'll know it when I see it."

Browse careers
by industry.

There are over 900 career options for
you to look at. Find yours in one of
these industries:

Administration & Support Services

Browse

"I'm not really sure."

Tell us what you
like to do.

Answer questions about the type of
work you might enjoy. We'll suggest
careers that match your interests and
training.

Start

Let's go through your choices and what each means. Remember, these are the four main choices:

- You believe you know EXACTLY which career is right for you.
- You don't know what career you want but you do know that you want to be in a particular industry.
- You don't have a clue about what you want to do.
- You are a veteran. [I discuss this later.]

Here is where it gets a little tricky. O*NET is organized by careers, which is about the "to do" part of your future. The self-assessment you have done is about who you are (to be). The challenge is for you to map from the who you are (to be) to what you will do in your career (to do). Along the way you will need to consider many dimensions of your career choice.

O*NET provides the information you need to decide. The "to do" information is buried in the O*NET data set. One of the first things you will see is how to access the "to do" of each career. But in the beginning you must begin your career evaluation with a career title because that is how the database is organized.

YOU BELIEVE YOU KNOW EXACTLY
WHICH CAREER IS RIGHT FOR YOU.

Don't forget that there are over 900 choices. You are choosing *one* of those careers to examine in depth. Go to the first choice on the left titled: "I want to be a ..." In the search box you see the phrase Search careers with key words. In the blank space enter the career you are interested in. For example, say that you want to be a Hospital Administrator. Enter *Hospital Administrator* in the empty box. Click the Search button below. Here is what you will see:

MY NEXT MOVE

Search results for
hospital administrator

Showing top 20 careers for **hospital administrator**. Closest matches are shown first.

Try another search:
hospital administrator

	Bright Outlook	green	Registered Apprenticeship
Medical & Health Services Managers			
Medical Records & Health Information Technicians			
Hospitalists			
First-Line Supervisors of Office & Administrative Support Workers			
Medical Secretaries			
Human Resources Managers			
Emergency Management Directors			
Food Servers, Nonrestaurant			
Librarians			
Maids & Housekeeping Cleaners			
Vocational Education Teachers, Postsecondary			
Receptionists & Information Clerks			
Food Preparation Workers			
Office Clerks, General			

Let's look at the first career listed. Click on Medical & Health Services Managers. You will see:

On this page are the major categories important to your decision on whether to be a Hospital Administrator. The first things listed are **What they do** and **On the job, you would**.

Although you may have started your search believing that you know exactly what you want to do, it is here where you need to have the first of your reality checks. Consider seriously the match between who you are and what you will do in this career. This is such an important step that I strongly recommend that you gain as much understanding about this career choice as possible.

On this web page you can see the major elements of the career (remember the screen shots here just show the top part of the online screen; you will need to scroll down to see all these elements):

KNOWLEDGE
SKILLS
ABILITIES
PERSONALITY
TECHNOLOGY
EDUCATION
JOB OUTLOOK
EXPLORE MORE

These are important to fully understand and evaluate your decision. But there is more involved in your decision. There is even more detailed information about a Hospital Administrator career. To get these details, open a second tab on your Internet browser. In that second tab enter the main web address. http://ficws.com/ONET You will see:

On this page click on Find Occupations. You will see

In the first gray bar in the left column you should see Keyword or O*NET-SOC Code. Directly under the title is an empty box. In that box enter *Hospital Administrator*. Click on **Go** in the oval to the right. You should see

The first line on this page shows the career you are exploring: **11-9111.00 Medical and Health Services Managers**. Click on **Medical and Health Services Managers**.

You will see

On this page, scroll down and read all of the elements of interest to you in this career. You now have very detailed information about a career as a Medical and Health Services Manager. These are the major categories:

Tasks
Tools & Technology
Knowledge
Skills
Abilities
Work Activities
Work Context
Job Zone
Education
Interests
Work Styles

Work Values
Related Occupations
Wages and Employment Trends
National: Includes
Median wages
Employment
Projected growth
Projected job openings
Top industries
State & National
Job Openings on the Web
Sources of Additional Information

On this page you can see important information related to the vision of your future that you created in chapter 3: Envision Your Future. In that chapter you thought about what you would enjoy doing in the future. On this page of Summary Report for 11-9111.00 Medical and Health Services Managers, scroll down to Work Activities in the gray bar. Here you see a great deal of detail about what you would be doing in a day in this career.

The major headings include the following:
Communication with Supervisors, Peers, or Subordinates
Making Decisions and Solving Problems
Establishing and Maintaining Interpersonal Relationships
Evaluating Information to Determine Compliance with
Standards
Developing and Building Teams
Getting Information
Monitoring and Controlling Resources
Analyzing Data or Information
Guiding, Directing, and Motivating Subordinates
Coordinating the Work and Activities of Others

This is the "to do" list of a typical day for you in the future were you to choose this career. It is very important that you are totally honest with yourself at this point. This is where the "to do" meets who you are in your future.

Scroll all the way to the bottom to the section Related Occupations in the gray bar near the bottom of this page. You will see

Click on 11-9032.00 Education Administrators, Elementary and Secondary School.

You will see this screen:

Scroll down to read all of the elements of 11-9032.00. This allows you to compare and contrast an administrative career in health care with an administrative career in education. In the first case, the administrative position is in health care, and in the other case the administration career is in education. It is wise to make this comparison on all of the fields for the two careers to make sure you know everything you need to know about the careers you are considering.

In the example we just looked at, you examined an administrative career in another industry (education). Let's look at another example. In this example you are not sure that you want to be an administrator, but you are absolutely certain that you want to have a career in the health care industry. Click back on the browser to return to the O*NET home page.

YOU DON'T KNOW WHAT CAREER YOU WANT BUT YOU DO KNOW THE PARTICULAR INDUSTRY.

Let's stay with the health care industry to build on our earlier work on Hospital Administrator. Open a third tab on your browser. Log onto O*NET. http://ficws.com/ONET
You will see

In the upper left corner click on **Find Occupations**.
You will see

In the left column you will see in the third area titled
Industry. Click on the dropdown menu arrow on the right
of the box under Industry. Click on Health Care and Social
Assistance. Then click on **Go** to the right of the box.
You will see

Scroll down the page. There are over a hundred careers listed in health care and related industries. Let's say you are interested in 31-9091.00 Dental Assistants. Click on the word Dental Assistants.

You will see

You are looking at precise details available for a Dental Assistant's career search similar to the one we did on the Hospital Administrator earlier. This level of detail is available for all of the health care careers listed. In fact, this level of detail is available for the 900+ careers inventoried on O*NET. It is up to you to select the career or industry that fits who you are. You have more than enough data to have one or more matches with your vision you created for yourself in chapter 3: Envision Your Future.

Click on Find Occupations at the top left of the page.

You will see

This screen shows several more ways to search. The categories are shown in the gray bars. These categories define additional ways to search for your ideal career. The searchable categories are these:

Keyword or O*NET-SOC Code
Career Cluster
Industry
Job Zone
Bright Outlook
Green Economy Sector
Job Family
STEM Discipline [Science, Technology, Engineering, and Mathematics]

All of these job categories are searched in the same way we searched the industry category previously. Of special interest here is the Job Zone. This searchable database tells you what careers are related to the level of education that every career requires. The Job Zone section can function as a form of career insurance policy. Here's how this works.

Let's say you select a career that requires a bachelor's degree or even a master's degree or a Ph.D. In this scenario, you chose your major and your school and you start out on the road to your degree. Then, let's do a "what if." What if something happens in your life that prevents you from completing your degree? Examples include the death of a spouse or the loss of your job.

If you recall, these are exactly the kinds of events that we looked at in chapter 4: You Have Competition for the Career You Want that caused people to drop out of school and not finish their degrees. Assume that you cannot continue studying for your original career choice.

In such a scenario, you will want to make the most out of the partial education you have been able to secure before the catastrophic event happened in your life. So you will want to search in the Job Zone dropdown menu to help you find a good back-up career that fits your current education level. As a nontraditional student with some education, you may even want to use this resource if you cannot return to school at this time.

Click on the arrow to the right of the box in Job Zone. You should see:

Job Zone

✓ One: Little or No Preparation Needed
Two: Some Preparation Needed
Three: Medium Preparation Needed
Four: Considerable Preparation Needed
Five: Extensive Preparation Needed
All Job Zones

;o

ive categories based on levels of
sary to perform the occupation.

Click on Two: Some Preparation Needed, then click on Go to the right of the box.

You should see

On this page you can look at the details about each career just as we did for Hospital Administrator.

Click on Find Occupations at the top left of the page. The other categories on this page are relatively obvious. For example, if you are really passionate about green and environmental issues, you will want to search in the Green Economy Sector. If you are good at math and science, you will want to thoroughly explore the STEM Discipline database. All of these categories link to the 900+ careers with all of the details that you saw in the Hospital Administrator example we explored earlier.

Oh, you don't know what you really want to do? Maybe your self-assessments weren't clear-cut. Or you want to look around at opportunities in your dream job. Let's do that now in the next section.

You don't have a clue
about what you want to do.

Let's go back to the beginning of the search and the home screen for O*NET. http://ficws.com/ONET The starting point for any of your searches is always who you are. As a complement to the recommended self-assessment inventories and the one you took in chapter 3: Envision Your Future, O*NET offers another software tool to help you determine who you are. Here is how to get to it and use it to your advantage.

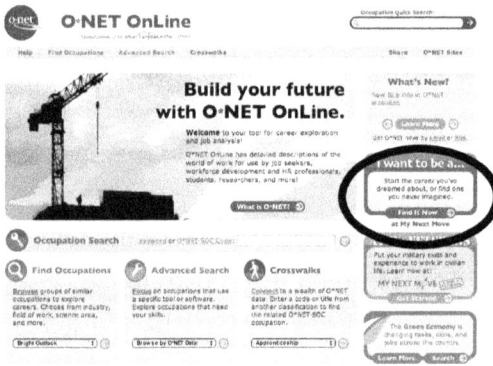

The box on the right is I want to be a ... Click on Find It Now in the bar at the bottom of the box.

You will see

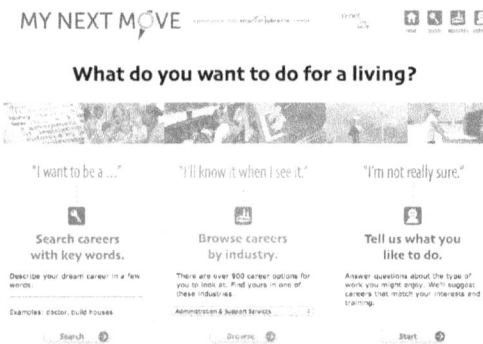

On the right you see "I'm not really sure." and below the text you see the box saying Tell us what you like to do. Click on Start.

You will see

Click on the Next arrow in the lower right. Read each screen and click Next to move ahead. Read the text on each screen and then continue to click on the Next arrow until you come to this screen:

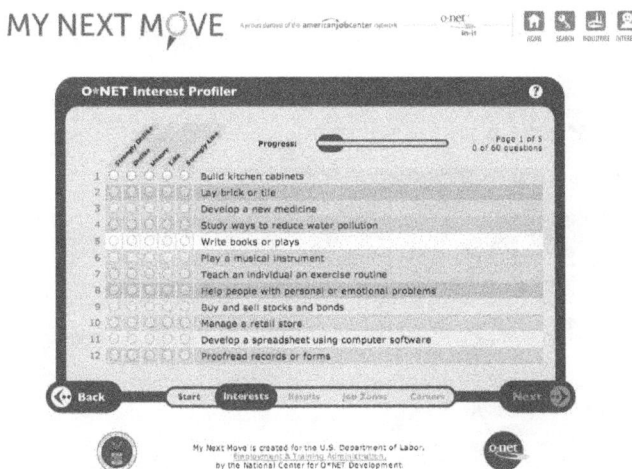

Complete all 60 questions. Follow the prompts until you reach the career section. Based on your responses, O*NET will respond with recommendations. The recommended careers screen looks like this, but remember, the recommended careers will be different for you than for the sample results shown here:

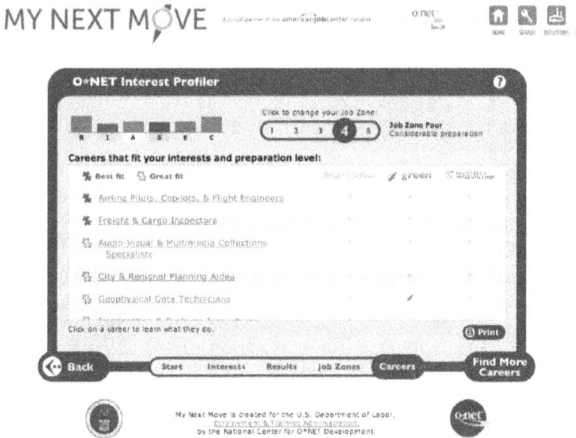

Click on the career choices that fit you. I clicked on Freight & Cargo Inspectors for this example.

You will see

Notice that this is the summary screen for careers. For more detail, go to the O*NET home page. http://ficws.com/ONET You will see

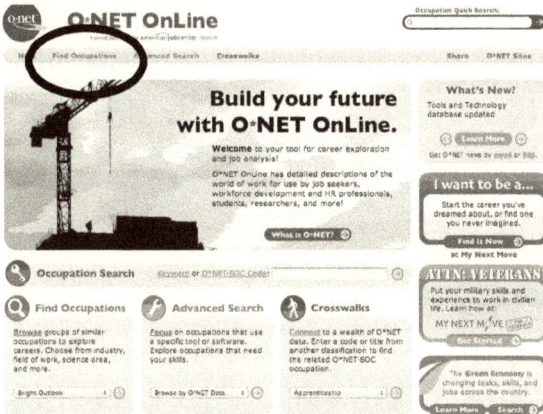

On the top left of the page click on **Find Occupations** and you will see

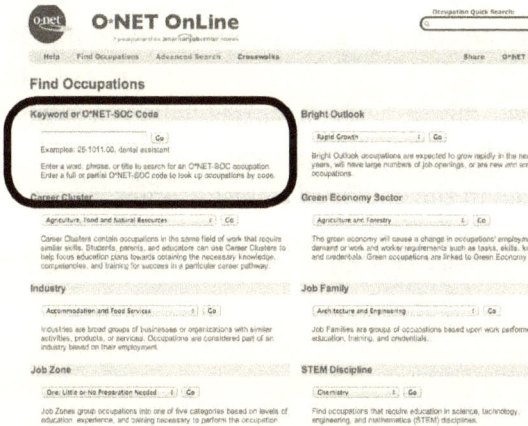

In the box for Keyword or O*NET-SOC Code, enter the career name you are interested in. The example I am using here is Freight & Cargo Inspectors. Click on **Go**. Here is what you will see for my example. Yours will be the same format

with different career choices depending on the answers you supplied in the O*NET Interest Profiler.

Here is what you should see (except yours will be different because the screen that actually comes up is based on who you are, which is exactly what we want to happen):

Click on the career you are interested in. In this example I clicked on Freight and Cargo Inspectors. Here is the screen you will see. All of these categories will be on your screen, but the details will depend on who you are and the answers you supplied in the O*NET Interest Profiler.

There is another way to identify careers that might fit
you. This approach builds on your current skills. Go back to
the main page. http://ficws.com/ONET Click on Advanced
Search in the middle top of the home page. You will see

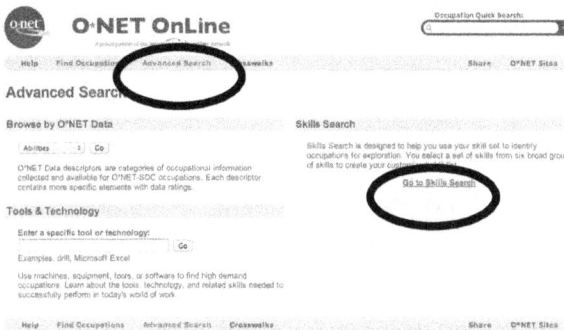

Under Skills Search in the gray bar, click on Go to Skills
Search on right side of the screen. You will see

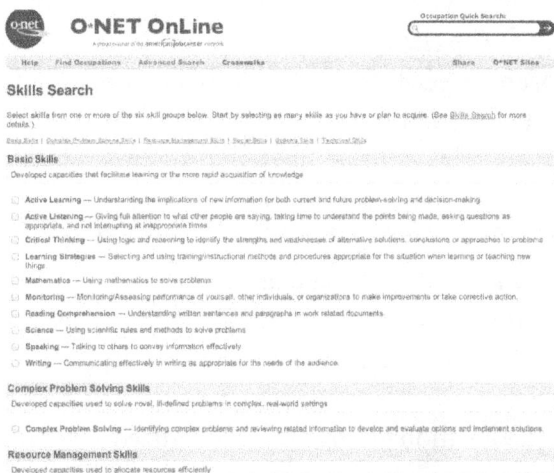

Check all the boxes for the skills you already have. This
will steer you to careers that you could qualify for right now.
After you submit your completed form, you will have access
to a listing of relevant jobs you can explore further.

Also try this search: Return to the Skills Search screen. This time enter your current skills and enter the skills that you plan to acquire with the completion of your degree. This search will return careers that you plan to be qualified for after you earn your degree.

THE MARRIAGE OF "COURSE OF STUDY" AND YOUR CAREER

We are now at the point of looking at courses of study that relate to the career choices you have made so far in this chapter.

O*NET has provided you with a far more comprehensive set of information than you ever had when you were a student just out of high school. With information about your skills, abilities, and interests, you are equipped to make an informed decision about what you should be studying in your chosen degree field. The challenge now is to match characteristics of your chosen career to education programs being offered by accredited universities.

Unfortunately, college degree programs do not map directly to the careers that are available in our modern economy. The fact is that the faculty of colleges and universities are not creating degree majors at the same rapid pace that the world economy is changing. This presents a challenge. You still have to choose an appropriate major for your career.

College education programs are organized around courses. Each course is most often three credits in length. Degree program names give only a rough idea what that specific program is about. Unfortunately, the names of courses tell even less about what the course content is.

The key document that you will need to review is each course's syllabus or summary. Once you have selected one or more universities to consider (more details about this in chapter 9: How to Pick the Right School), you can match the syllabus for each course in your major with the skills and abilities you identified in your selected career. This portion of your project will require additional investment of your time and energy. Stay with it. It will be worth it.

Here are examples of a course description or syllabus for each of two different occupations. If they look familiar, they are. We discussed these two jobs earlier in this chapter. It's important to ask for this level of detail when you talk to any university. If the university will not supply you with this level of detail about its programs, then pursue other universities that will provide the detail you seek.

Computer and Information Systems Manager

Course: Installing, Configuring and Administering Microsoft Windows Operating Systems.

Prerequisites: None

Credit: 4 Credit Hours

Catalog Description: This course introduces students to knowledge and skills related to maintaining the most current version of Microsoft Windows Operating System. This course provides a foundation of networking concepts and contrasts the different types of networking structures. This class introduces the concepts of administration of local and wide area networks. Where possible, course materials are aligned with coursework that prepares students for the Microsoft certification exam for Installing, Configuring and Administrating Microsoft Operating Systems.

Purpose: The purpose of this course is to prepare students for the entry-level administration jobs in systems administration and technologies. In addition, non-technical professionals can enhance their knowledge of the administration of desktop users and operating systems software.

Objectives: Students who successfully complete this course should be able to:

1. Explain operating systems installation and boot processes.
2. Demonstrate ability to manage operating systems configuration and security.
3. Demonstrate ability to manage operating systems desktop environments and mobile computing.
4. Identify methods of troubleshooting networking problems and security issues.

Course Outline:

Installing a Desktop Operating System

A. Manually installing Windows Desktop Operating System
B. Automating a Windows Desktop Operating System
C. Transferring user files and settings to a new computer
D. Using an image to install Windows Desktop Operating System

Marriage and Family Therapist

Course: Using Critical Thinking to Understand Human Behavior

Prerequisites: None

Credit: 3 Credit Hours

Catalog Description: This course applies critical thinking skills to human behavior. Topics include the self in society; truth versus belief; human nature and its origin; love, sex, and friendship; personal and social morality; learning and creativity; work and recreation; law; government, democracy, change and progress, war and peace, thoughts about God and hope for the future.

Purpose: This course is a critical investigation into human nature, origins, values, emotion, and behavior. It may be used to satisfy three credits of the general education core requirements in either Human Behavior or Human Thought or three elective credits toward graduation.

Objectives: Students who successfully complete this course will be able to:

1. Analyze important considerations concerning truth, opinion, learning, art and knowledge.
2. Criticize the major theories of human origins and human nature.
3. Characterize the importance of human emotion, love, friendship, and sex in human behavior.
4. Assess central claims about the nature of human freedom, government, law, punishment, and justice.
5. Analyze the great dyads in human life: good and evil, change and progress, work and play, justice and mercy, freedom and responsibility, war and peace, and science and religion.

Course outline:

Analysis of Important Considerations Concerning Truth, Opinion, Learning, Art and Knowledge

A. How to think about truth
B. How to think about opinion

In summary, make sure that your college degree major consists of courses that best match your career interests. The critical documents to consider in this decision are the course descriptions, particularly for your degree major. Requesting and then reviewing this information helps you understand the purpose and objectives of the courses you need to take.

Deciding on which career and major you want to pursue are important considerations when returning to college to complete your degree. While you are finishing your degree, there are other activities you can become involved in to help you prepare for re-entering the job market and/or pursuing a new career.

- Join professional associations (such as the American Society of Civil Engineers, if that's related to your interests) or attend related conferences and events. These networking activities can be engaging and informative.
- Participate in professional meetings in your selected career to make you more aware of who the top professionals are in the field you are studying.
- Take advantage of networking opportunities. They build confidence, make you more knowledgeable, and give you an inside track when it comes to seeking employment after finishing your degree.
- Resources can be found online and at local libraries (both public and academic) to assist you in locating these associations, conferences, and meetings.
- Become a presence on the professional social networking site LinkedIn.

MAKE YOUR CHOICE FIT YOU

By selecting a field of study and ultimately a career based on who you are as a person, you are accentuating your strengths and passions. A career choice is about what you are going to do daily in your work life. It's like buying a new pair of shoes. It's important that you make the choice that fits you. Whether it fits someone else is irrelevant to you.

ACTION STEPS

- Reflect on how you made the last decision to get an education. Place the following elements in the order you considered them the last time: who you are, what career best fits you, the university you selected, and your major course of study. Then consider how these elements are different today.
- Reach out to a traditional university near you and ask a recruiter what he or she thinks are the three most important benefits of an education at the institution you contacted. These responses need to be about you, your career, and your job opportunities, not what that university can do for you.
- Put in the time. Do the O*NET exercises in the chapter.
- Looking back to the time before you performed the O*NET research, what were the two most attractive careers to you? Now list the two most attractive careers to you after completing the exercises in this chapter. Are they the same? Document why these are careers are attractive to you.
- Get the course descriptions for two courses at a university you are considering attending.

■　■　■

09

HOW TO PICK THE RIGHT SCHOOL

More than 6,500 American institutions provide post-secondary education in the United States. While this means you have many colleges and universities from which to select, the decision can be just as overwhelming as picking your major.

Consider these factors when you are deciding which college or university you plan to attend to earn your degree:

- The total cost of your degree: list and net tuition price
- Availability of the major and course of study that fits who you are
- Regional accreditation (Note: Regional accreditation is the highest quality certification recognized by the U.S. Department of Education.)
- Geographic location
- The size of the student body
- The potential to study online
- Quality, convenience, accessibility, and support services including financial aid and academic counseling

In this chapter I will help you sort through a valuable database created and maintained by the research arm of the U.S. Department of Education. This database contains information on universities and is continually updated to include the most current information available.

I strongly encourage you to read each section and do the exercises, even if the example included is not about your selected career. The content provided builds on the basic ideas from section to section and will be valuable to you as you journey to earning your degree.

TRADITIONAL CAMPUS OR ONLINE UNIVERSITY?

In America, education has been viewed as an important factor in creating value and improving society and the lives of individual citizens. As a result, tax dollars have been allocated to fund colleges and universities so they can make higher education affordable for our citizens. Tax subsidies have been targeted at education for the young—most notably, recent high school graduates. These educational opportunities come in the form of traditional public universities that were designed for resident education where students take courses on a physical campus. Even today, those courses are often delivered in a lecture format where understanding the content of the course is the most important learning objective.

Innovative technology combined with society's recognition of the need for lifelong learning has created a new market.. This market includes online for-profit educational institutions serving adult learners like you. These universities provide convenience and flexibility. The mission of traditional universities is to educate young people. In contrast, the mission of for-profit universities is to produce a financial return for their stockholders. The entrance of for-profit universities into higher education presents adult learners with more viable options for getting their degrees.

Obviously, there is greater flexibility and choice with online education. When taking courses online it is not necessary to go to the campus to access the library, sit in class, or take proctored exams. As a student of an online nontraditional university, you can complete the activities on your schedule and at your selected place through an Internet connection.

The biggest issue about online degrees is the quality of the learning. There is third party scientific research on the issue. The U.S. Department of Education has done extensive research comparing online learning to traditional face-to-face learning. Their research concludes that "on average, students in online learning conditions performed modestly better than those receiving face-to-face instruction." (Reference: U.S. Department of Education, Evaluation of Evidence-Based Practices in Online Learning, A Meta Analysis and Review of Online Learning Studies, revised September, 2010, p. ix)

If the cost of an institution is equal to or less than a qualified face-to-face alternative university, the argument for learning online is compelling. This does not mean that the quality of every online learning experience is better than the quality of every face-to-face learning experience. The quality of individual courses and programs varies greatly from institution to institution. Selecting the right university for quality is still a challenge.

Also, remember that some learners simply learn better in a physical campus setting. This has more to do with the individual's learning style than the characteristics of the college or university. In other words, when it comes to online versus in class it is as much about who you are as it is about the college or university.

From the Department of Education research and the millions of adult learners learning online, it is safe to say that online learning is a highly viable alternative for you to consider for your degree. Investigate it.

A SOURCE OF INFORMATION YOU WILL NEED—UNIVERSITY ENROLLMENT DEPARTMENTS

Universities that serve adult learners have invested in comprehensive systems and processes to help their nontraditional students make enrollment decisions. Enrollment counselors serve as personal advisors to prospective students like you, but it is important to remember that they are representing the interests of the institution they work for. Their goal is to get you to register with them.

Enrollment counselors provide answers about the school itself, programs, courses, admission tests required, services, costs, and other areas of university operations. In addition, good enrollment counselors provide information about financial matters, including scholarships, federal loan guarantees, financial aid, Pell Grants, and other financing options.

In this financial advisory capacity, they are trained to help you put together the personal money plan you need to finance your education. Not everyone qualifies, but to know if you do, you will need their advice and counsel. Academic advisors are also available for direct conversations about courses and degree programs. The enrollment counselor will give you access to academic advisors in those cases where more course and degree program information is required.

The risk is that once you connect with a particular university for these enrollment services, the information provided is biased by the interests of that university. In a sense, the prospective student becomes captive to the specific university giving them advice and counsel. Because the university is the source of the advice, it may not be an objective broker of the information. Admission counselors are highly motivated to give lots of information about what I call the "within" issues. That is, they are professionals highly knowledgeable about their university. They are also motivated to do whatever is necessary to get you to enroll. They are neither knowledgeable nor motivated to inform you about your decision "between" universities. This is one of the reasons I recommended earlier that you not start with the selection of the university as the first decision you make. More on this later in this chapter.

The institution has a compelling interest to enroll you, the prospective student, in order to capture the revenue. This is especially true of for-profit universities.

For-profit universities are exactly what their name says. They are for profit. On the other hand, nonprofit universities are much more focused on their mission and are less driven by the need to generate earnings the way for-profit universities are. My only advice on this is that the mission of any institution impacts the behavior of the individuals in that organization, but I will leave the final decision to you. In all of your choices you should ask about the university's mission and try to understand the balance between the mission and the money at that particular university.

If you were buying a car, you'd get basic information given with a certain biased opinion from the interests of the car salesperson at the dealership. At a university that person is the enrollment counselor. But if you also look at objective sources for information on the model of car you wish to buy—from *Consumer Reports* or *Kelly Blue Book*, for example—you can gather enough unbiased information to make a better decision. Ironically, buying a car has less impact on your future than deciding on which university to attend. Yet you can get more objective information about the car purchase. The more important university decision has little objective information about price, quality and prior customer experiences.

One of my goals in this book is to be much more like *Consumer Reports* than like a car salesperson. This is one of the reasons I want you to spend time understanding what is in this book *before* you speak to the car salesperson, i.e. the enrollment counselor.

It is important for you to have objective third-party information about college costs and programs before contacting any university. A good source of such objective information is available at the U.S. Department of Education's National Center for Education Statistics website called COLLEGENavigator.

Just as O*NET provides information about career choices, COLLEGENavigator provides comprehensive data about all accredited colleges and universities in the United States. This includes nonprofit, for-profit, traditional, and online. The challenge is to help you navigate this vast amount of information to make the right choices for you. The rest of this chapter does just that.

LET'S EXPLORE COLLEGENAVIGATOR

As was the case in the career selection decisions on O*NET, I recommend using an unbiased third-party database to select the right school to attend. The data on COLLEGENavigator is continually updated to include the most current information on institutions of higher education.

Here is the template for the information contained for each institution you might consider.

Bellevue University
1000 Galvin Rd S, Bellevue, Nebraska 68005-3098

General information:	(402) 291-8100
Website:	bellevue.edu
Type:	4-year, Private not-for-profit
Awards offered:	Bachelor's degree
	Master's degree
	Doctor's degree - research/scholarship
Campus setting:	Suburb: Large
Campus housing:	No
Student population:	10,407 (7,245 undergraduate)
Student-to-faculty ratio:	23 to 1

IPEDS ID: 180814
OPE ID: 00974300

Expand All   Collapse All

- GENERAL INFORMATION
- TUITION, FEES, AND ESTIMATED STUDENT EXPENSES
- FINANCIAL AID
- NET PRICE
- ENROLLMENT
- ADMISSIONS
- RETENTION AND GRADUATION RATES
- PROGRAMS/MAJORS
- VARSITY ATHLETIC TEAMS
- ACCREDITATION
- CAMPUS SECURITY
- COHORT DEFAULT RATES

Each of the categories listed is a clickable Internet link with details provided on the actual website.

Four separate sections of this chapter explore the main considerations for you to think about when selecting and comparing any college or university. These include topics related to your specific needs such as:

- You know your major and total cost is a primary factor.
- You have a limited budget and you need to get the lowest cost.
- Discounts: I want to know about list versus net pricing at American colleges and universities.
- Money to be saved: What is the credit transfer policy including prior learning experience?

To get the most out of this chapter, read each section and complete the exercises.

YOU KNOW YOUR MAJOR AND TOTAL
COST IS NOT A PRIMARY FACTOR.

For the majority of students, cost is an important factor. I start with this section however, to establish a "base case" for understanding the data available. I also introduce several key decision factors in this example.

Open two tabs on your web browser. In the first tab, go to the home page for COLLEGENavigator.
http://nces.ed.gov/collegenavigator/
You will see

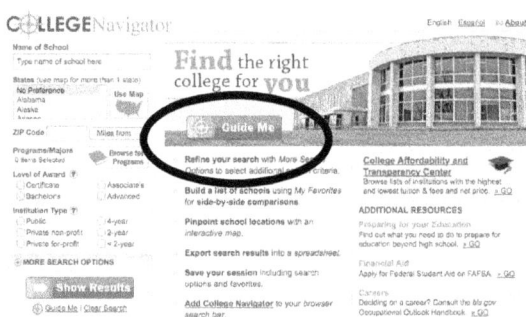

Notice that there is a Guide Me block on the web page. I am going to navigate the data in a different way than recommended by Guide Me. I am going to show you how to build your college alternatives based upon who you are and the career that fit you. So let's start with your selected career choice from the last chapters and find colleges and universities that offer programs that prepare you for that career. From there, we will look at other school factors including location, cost, and more.

Let's return to the three example careers we initially identified in an earlier chapter:

- Computer and Information Systems Manager
- Marriage and Family Therapist
- Graphic Designer

Our example search within COLLEGENavigator is for Graphic Designer. Look at the COLLEGENavigator home page opened in the first tab of your Internet browser. In the left-hand column under the title COLLEGENavigator scroll down to the box with the book icon titled **Browse for Programs** and click it.

In the **Programs/Majors** box in your browser that says "Type your keyword here," type Graphic Design and hit the **Search** button. You will see

Click on **+add** in the line **+add Graphic Design** to move that to the upper box. Click on **Show Results**. You are now looking at over 500 institutions that offer graphic design programs in the United States. At this point you have the option to select any of the search options under the COLLEGENavigator section.

You have, of course, the same capability to search any of the careers (or any not on that list as well) including the Marriage and Family Therapist career we looked at in an earlier chapter.

NOTE: Always remember to Clear Search at the bottom of the COLLEGENavigator column before looking at a new career/program. If you don't, you might artificially restrict your options too early in your search. The key is to always go from broad to narrow as you consider any of the factors in your program selection.

YOU HAVE A LIMITED BUDGET AND
YOU NEED TO GET THE BEST VALUE.

Now you have an idea about how to move around the COLLEGENavigator website. Let's examine the financial and geographic factors in your decision. For demonstration purposes, we will use a career in Graphic Design.

In this scenario we are assuming that you cannot afford to enroll directly in a four-year bachelor's-degree program but instead plan to go to a two-year community college first and then transfer to a four-year institution to complete your degree. You may decide to do this because you want to live at home to save expenses or you may be working and are unable to move to get your education. These are some of the reasons that a choice like Harvard University is just not a realistic alternative for you.

This example also assumes that you live in Mendota Heights, Minnesota (ZIP code 55150), and you want face-to-face classes delivered in a classroom. In face-to-face learning delivered at a physical location, the state of your residency is important.

Taxpayers in each state subsidize their public colleges and universities. This makes for large differences between resident and non-resident tuition costs. Where you live and where you decide to go to school can significantly impact your costs, especially if you plan to go to a state-supported public institution.

In this Mendota Heights example, let's assume you are willing to commute from home a maximum of twenty-five miles one way to go to class. This distance factor will be especially important if you are working full time. One of the last things you want to do is spend hours commuting to and from class. This also is a key geographic factor if you are engaging in face-to-face learning. If you decide to study online, you have much more flexibility.

Go to COLLEGENavigator. http://nces.ed.gov/collegenavigator/ Enter the ZIP code in the ZIP Code box as 55150. Obviously, you'll enter your own ZIP code when you do your searches. In this example indicate you'll travel twenty-five miles in the Miles From dropdown box.

Click MORE SEARCH OPTIONS. In the dropdown box that says Maximum under Tuition and Fees, select $5,000.

Click on Browse for Programs. In the Programs/Majors box in your browser that says "Type your keyword here," type Graphic Design and hit the Search button. Click on +add in the line +add Graphic Design to move that to the upper box. Click on Show Results.

You will see

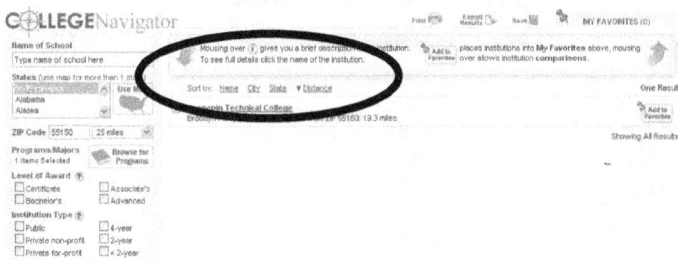

What you are looking at is the choices within twenty-five miles of ZIP code 55150 that have a Graphic Design program with annual tuition of $5,000 or less. This gives you a base case to reference in your college choice decision. Now you'd want to look at more details about Hennepin Technical College.

Click on **Hennepin Technical College.** Under **TUITION, FEES, AND ESTIMATED STUDENT EXPENSES** you can see that the 2012–2013 tuition and fees meet our $5,000 limit at $4,998. But there is also an estimated total cost of $2,000 dollars of books and supplies, bringing the total annual cost to $6,998 per year while living at home. Of course this total does not include living costs if you plan to actually become a resident student who lives in a new location on or near the university.

Let's explore some further options for an associate's degree in Graphic Design.

We will keep all the previous parameters the same, but increase the annual budget to $25,000 for tuition. Under **Institution Type,** select a degree program from either a two-year or four-year institutions. Enter these selections and then click on **Show Results.**

You will see

Click on Academy College. On this page, you can see that Academy College is within 6.6 miles from the Mendota Heights residence and you can work on an associate's degree or you can work directly on your bachelor's degree. The total annual cost at Academy College for tuition and books was $21,323 per year in 2012–2013 versus $6,998 at Hennepin Technical College. The decision you need to make in this choice is whether the other features and aspects of Academy College justify the $14,325 additional cost Academy College commands in the market for Graphic Design degrees over that are offered by Hennepin Technical College.

In one last look at Graphic Design, let's look at how much you could conceivably spend on a four-year degree. In this search select Bachelor's, 4-year, private non-profit with no monetary cap on tuition and no commute distance restrictions. This search provides hundreds of results.

A random selection from these results is Boston University in Boston, Massachusetts. Click on TUITION, FEES, AND ESTIMATED STUDENT EXPENSES.

In the section titled Estimated Expenses for Academic Year, the column 2012-2013, you will see that tuition and fees are $42,994 and books and supplies are $1,000. This shows that enrolling in the Boston University Graphic Design program for 2012–2013 has a total cost for tuition and fees, books, and supplies of $43,994 per year.

It is clear from these comparisons that the cost to study Graphic Design varies tremendously. At the low end, we have an annual cost of $6,998 per year for an associate degree at Hennepin Technical College in Minnesota versus $43,994 at Boston University in Massachusetts. These numbers make it clear that the university choice warrants your best effort before you select a university to get your degree.

Additional data on each institution is available on the COLLEGENavigator site. It is important to explore all of the data for each school you are seriously considering.

DISCOUNTS: LIST VERSUS NET PRICING AT AMERICAN COLLEGES AND UNIVERSITIES.

Most American universities discount the price of tuition by offering institutional scholarships and grants. They do this because competition is increasing among colleges and universities. Offering scholarships is a branding strategy and a clever way to offer a lower price without calling it a discount. A scholarship is money paid toward your "bill" that you don't have to pay back. It is not a loan.

A merit scholarship is far more appealing than calling the resulting net amount a "price discount." No matter what it is called, in the end it is about how much it is going to cost you. To some people, a "price discount" sounds cheap while a merit scholarship sounds prestigious.

The use of scholarships to make an institution more price competitive has become widespread. These practices make it important that you understand the true price at the particular institution before you decide to pursue your degree there. COLLEGENavigator provides the price data needed to compare different universities on a cost basis. Also, this website helps you establish your negotiating position with the institution(s) of your choice. In this economy, it is important to shop around!

Go to the COLLEGENavigator home page. http://nces.ed.gov/collegenavigator/ I have randomly selected a different institution to compare in the list versus actual tuition cost.

To find the data used in this section, enter the name of the university in the first box under **Name of School** shown directly under COLLEGENavigator. I have entered the name of one institution, in this case Fairleigh Dickinson University–College at Florham. Click on **Fairleigh Dickinson University–College at Florham** on the right. You can actually do this search online or just follow along on these pages.

You should see this information about this school in New Jersey:

Fairleigh Dickinson University-College at Florham
285 Madison Ave, Madison, New Jersey 07940

General information:	(973) 443-8500
Website:	www.fdu.edu
Type:	4-year, Private not-for-profit
Awards offered:	Bachelor's degree
	Postbaccalaureate certificate
	Master's degree
	Post-master's certificate
	Doctor's degree - professional practice
Campus setting:	Suburb: Large
Campus housing:	Yes
Student population:	3,082 (2,401 undergraduate)
Student-to-faculty ratio:	12 to 1

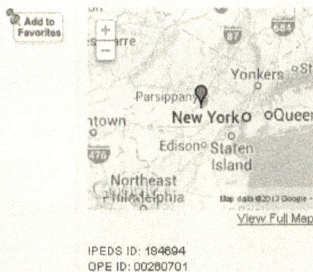

Add to Favorites

IPEDS ID: 184694
OPE ID: 00280701

View Full Map

Expand All   Collapse All

⊕ GENERAL INFORMATION

⊕ TUITION, FEES, AND ESTIMATED STUDENT EXPENSES

⊕ FINANCIAL AID

⊕ NET PRICE

⊕ ENROLLMENT

⊕ ADMISSIONS

⊕ RETENTION AND GRADUATION RATES

⊕ PROGRAMS/MAJORS

⊕ VARSITY ATHLETIC TEAMS

⊕ ACCREDITATION

⊕ CAMPUS SECURITY

To look at scholarship information, we need to look under the FINANCIAL AID section.

FINANCIAL AID

UNDERGRADUATE STUDENT FINANCIAL AID, 2010-2011

Full-time Beginning Undergraduate Students
- Beginning students are those who are entering postsecondary education for the first time.

TYPE OF AID	NUMBER RECEIVING AID	PERCENT RECEIVING AID	TOTAL AMOUNT OF AID RECEIVED	AVERAGE AMOUNT OF AID RECEIVED
Any student financial aid[1]	636	99%	—	—
Grant or scholarship aid	634	98%	$13,129,699	$20,709
Federal grants	229	36%	$1,223,055	$5,341
Pell grants	227	35%	$987,739	$4,351
Other federal grants	191	30%	$235,316	$1,232
State/local government grant or scholarships	203	32%	$1,604,366	$7,903
Institutional grants or scholarships	631	98%	$10,302,278	$16,327
Student loan aid	510	79%	$5,373,904	$10,537
Federal student loans	505	78%	$3,011,506	$5,963
Other student loans	127	20%	$2,362,398	$18,602

- [1] Includes students receiving Federal work study aid and aid from other sources not listed above.

All Undergraduate Students

TYPE OF AID	NUMBER RECEIVING AID	PERCENT RECEIVING AID	TOTAL AMOUNT OF AID RECEIVED	AVERAGE AMOUNT OF AID RECEIVED
Grant or scholarship aid[1]	2,094	86%	$38,151,585	$18,219
Pell grants	895	28%	$3,016,423	$4,340

If you look under **All Undergraduate Students**, you will see that 86% of undergraduate students received a grant or scholarship aid in 2010-2011. You can also see under AVERAGE AMOUNT OF AID RECEIVED that in 2010-2011, the average amount of aid by the institution was $18,219.

All Undergraduate Students

TYPE OF AID	NUMBER RECEIVING AID	PERCENT RECEIVING AID	TOTAL AMOUNT OF AID RECEIVED	AVERAGE AMOUNT OF AID RECEIVED
Grant or scholarship aid[1]	2,094	86%	$38,151,585	$18,219
Pell grants	695	28%	$3,016,423	$4,340
Federal student loans	1,609	66%	$10,951,282	$6,808

Student grants are free monetary gifts to people who are pursuing higher education. Unlike student loans, grants do not require repayment. Student grants also differ from scholarships, which are usually given to and by specific groups of people for a specific line of study and often require students to have exceptional grades. Scholarships are also free money that does not have to be paid back.

Public universities typically do less discounting in the form of institutional grants and scholarships. But if you are considering attending a state university as a non-resident of that state, it is important that you ask the average price paid by non-residents. That specific data for public institutions is not available on COLLEGENavigator; only data representing the total for the combined resident and non-resident entering student are available.

It is important for you to know the relationship between net price and list price for tuition for any and every college/ university you are seriously considering. Universities will not volunteer a price discount (scholarship). *You have to ask*. Furthermore, if one university knows that you have a better offer from a competitor, this institution may be more likely to offer a merit scholarship. *Be prepared to negotiate the net price of your education*. Yes, it sounds a bit unusual and below the grandeur of "higher" education, but that's the reality.

You have to be a smart, informed consumer of education services—just as you would research and price buying a car or a flat-screen TV—to look out for your own interests when it comes to college costs. Review the COLLEGENavigator data for each institution before you begin your negotiations over the actual price you eventually pay. Yes, your college costs are negotiable.

A logical question in this discussion is, "When do I ask about the availability of merit scholarships and whom do I ask?" My recommendation is that you leave the merit scholarship conversation until after you have been admitted and are reasonably certain this particular university is a serious candidate under consideration. In other words, the price discount negotiation is one of the last things you do before you make your final choice. It does not take place at the beginning.

You actually want to tell your contact at the university, "I am seriously considering attending your school, but there is just one more thing that needs to be resolved." At this point you need to tell your contact that their institution is one of the two or three finalists in your enrollment decision and that you are asking each of those institutions what is available in the form of scholarships if you do enroll.

Your contact will know exactly what this conversation is about, and that representative is empowered by the organization to have that conversation. Press on until you get a definitive answer in writing. This conversation needs to take place with the admissions office or your enrollment counselor.

The bottom line is that you have to be prepared to negotiate if you want to get the lowest cost at the institution of your choice. As we have seen, there are lots of choices for your education. To get the best return on your education investment, you need to work hard at the beginning to get the most favorable investment cost for your education.

By referencing the material in this chapter you can get a good idea about what each college or university offers in the way of discounts—on average. This gives you important information on the minimum tuition reduction that is possible.

You will never know if you actually got the best deal possible. What is important is that you know the comparisons *among* institutions, and yes it is perfectly acceptable, just as in any comparison shopping, to tell one institution what another has already offered.

Most people do not look at education as a market with buyers and sellers. You need to. In the end, education is a high-cost purchase. Like buying a house or a car, you need to have access to objective data, such as this book and the willingness to shop around and negotiate when you get near a decision.

MONEY TO BE SAVED

What is the credit transfer policy including prior learning experience? There are additional possibilities that have the potential to further reduce the cost of your education. You are accumulating credits, like building a path (this is your journey to a degree), and each brick on that path is a semester credit. Your goal is to have 120 total semester credits to reach the end of your path and graduate.

One technical side note is important at this stage. Some colleges are on a quarter system and others are on a semester system. This is a very important standard for you to have to compare options at various universities. To add even more confusion, some colleges report the tuition costs for courses instead of credit hours. Typically a course will be one to five semester credit hours with three semester credit hours being most typical.

Some will talk about courses; some will talk about credit hours. Always keep in mind that it takes at least 120 semester credit hours to earn a regionally accredited bachelor's degree in the United States. Do not be confused by comments about cost of courses or quarter credit hours. A quarter hour is about 60 percent of a semester credit hour. It is critical for you to understand your costs and your degree credit hour requirements in standard semester credit hours. Apples to apples.

Here is your blueprint for the yellow brick road to a bachelor's degree. It shows the general path and what it means to earn the credits required for a bachelor's degree.

THE YELLOW BRICK ROAD
TO YOUR DEGREE

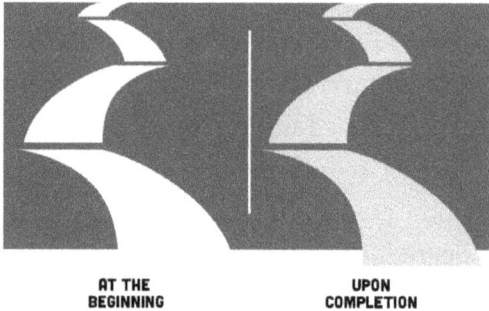

AT THE BEGINNING   **UPON COMPLETION**

On the left we see your path before you have any credits toward your degree. You are without any yellow bricks. On the right you see the pathway when you have enough credits (yellow bricks) to reach your goal for a bachelor's degree.

In the traditional freshman through senior education model, high school graduates start at the same place. Typically they have no credits (assets or bricks) to consider unless they have taken Advanced Placement (AP) courses in high school. For an entering freshman, the path is set and the student progresses in a predictable path from brick to brick (course by course). For example, the freshman English course is followed by Advanced Composition, and so on.

The education model is built for students to move from brick to brick along the path because they have no experience or reason to do otherwise. The path is well defined with few options.

Also, in the traditional higher education model, parents of college students typically pay for their child's education. Because you are an adult, however, you get to pay your own way. It is important that you purchase wisely.

The path to an accredited bachelor's degree in America begins with the general education core. Later will be the path to your major. Within this section are the classes specific to the degree you are pursuing. For the most part, there is little flexibility in the courses needed to fulfill the requirements of this part of your degree program.

These two elements (core and major classwork) are required by the regional accrediting bodies of American higher education. There are a total of approximately 72 credits required for both the general education core and your major area of study. The balance of credits taken toward a degree is called electives. Here, students have a variety of choices.

- *General education core.* Let's look at your journey to earn your degree. Consider your path as a game where you collect bricks to build your road. For traditional college freshmen, general education courses are taken at the beginning of the degree path. This gives new college students a solid foundation for later study. This is particularly important for students going directly from high school to college. These students have little life experience and need a solid academic foundation to build upon as they later study more complex subjects.

Unlike traditional college students, you do not have to take the general education core first. You can fill in your bricks in a different sequence, and, indeed, with many adult learners, some of these requirements are actually filled last.

Additionally, with adult learners there are a number of ways the path can be built. For instance, if you previously attended a traditional undergraduate program, you probably completed some general education courses since they are most often offered in the freshman and sophomore years.

In American universities the university you are going to, not the university you are coming from, sets the policies for accepting credits (bricks) from other colleges and universities. Thus, the number of bricks you qualify for depends upon the university to which you are going, not the university you left.

In other words, let's assume you completed some courses at the first school you attended. The institution you go to complete your degree will make the decision as to which credits will transfer. Let's say you are considering two universities and submit your transcript with your previously completed courses to both. Your yellow bricks (accepted credits) for prospective University A and University B may look like this:

PRIOR ACCREDITED COLLEGE COURSES
EXAMPLE: 12 3-CREDIT COURSES

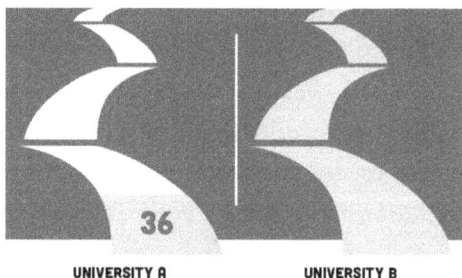

UNIVERSITY A   UNIVERSITY B

- *Electives.* The mid-section of your yellow brick path represents the electives. This section provides you with more options to earn more yellow bricks to complete your road to your degree. It is a large section with about 48 bricks and another area where your selection of a college or university has a big impact on your journey and the costs to reach your degree.

As always, you can earn yellow bricks by taking courses offered by your selected college. Yet you have more options than in the general education core section. In that section, the bricks you brought with you were purchased at another accredited university. In the electives section of the path, you may bring some yellow bricks to the path; however, just as with the first section, what you can bring depends upon the university you are going to, not the university you are coming from.

For an example, let's assume you work for an organization that provides lots of corporate training. Or perhaps you are a military veteran or you have had some special certification like those programs provided by Cisco or Microsoft. Some of this training may qualify as one or more yellow bricks in the elective section.

Here again we look at two different universities. If you have already had a discussion with a particular university that accepted your general education credits, then continue to explore the electives section with them to take full advantage of the bricks you already have.

Here is how the electives section might look at our two universities:

CREDIT FOR LIFE EXPERIENCE
AND OTHER EDUCATION

UNIVERSITY E   UNIVERSITY F

The universities in this figure have similar implications. University F is more likely to be a "highly selective" university than is University E.

Unfortunately this dimension of selectivity in American higher education has become linked with perceived quality. In general, the more restrictive a particular university transfer policy, the more selective and thus the more it is perceived as being of higher quality.

In the case of student admissions, highly selective universities, such as Harvard University, have the luxury of admitting only the most qualified applicants. This selectivity of student acceptance at Harvard is most valuable to employers because those who hire the graduates of such programs know that the university has rigorously screened their students.

For the employer of the graduates this makes it much more likely that the student being interviewed upon graduation is among the best and the brightest because that was a selection criterion upon entry. This concentration of talent in the interviewing process has market value to the hiring company. Higher offering salaries at least in part reflect this value, which in turn reinforces the prestige of the awarded degree. It is not all about the students who attend, but the selectivity around their original selection is one reason these graduates command such regard, both economically and socially.

As a result, it is true that being accepted by Harvard University is a good indicator that the admitted student is bright and highly qualified to benefit from the unique resources of Harvard University. In this example, high selectivity is an indication of the high quality of the *student body*.

COMMUNITY COLLEGES

There is another important type of learning institution that can help you cost effectively earn additional bricks for your road in a timely and cost-efficient way. These are our community colleges. We have already looked at the list tuition costs of a community college versus a four-year degree institution. But there is another dimension to this community college decision.

Deciding to attend a community college first is an attractive option that potentially allows you to efficiently complete sections of your path.

More so than ever before, community colleges are garnering much attention at the national level. The Bill and Melinda Gates Foundation, The Aspen Institute, and Corporate Voices for Working Families all have made community colleges a high priority for addressing the nation's education challenges. They became a focus at the national level because of their convenience, diversity of offerings, and cost-effectiveness.

Community colleges provide individual courses and award two-year associate's degrees. They cover two areas of education:

1. They provide specialized courses intended to develop specific marketable skills such as automotive technology, welding, and numerical controlled machine tool programming.
2. They provide "gen ed" (general education) courses. These are the courses typically taken in the first two years at a traditional university.

Because community colleges are generally tax supported, the tuition at these institutions typically is significantly lower than the tuition at public or private four-year institutions as we have already seen. A community college choice is also practical when the career selected (see chapter 7: How to Pick the Right Career for You) requires only an associate's degree as designated in O*NET.

In this example selectivity is a consideration in the tradeoff between cost and quality.

COMMUNITY COLLEGE
ASSOCIATE DEGREE TRANSFER

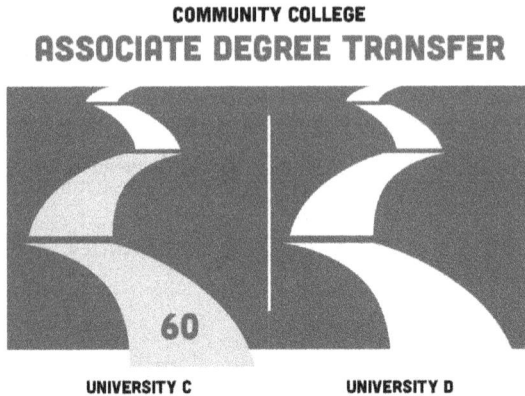

UNIVERSITY C   UNIVERSITY D

University C accepts a community college associate's degree while university D does not accept the associate's degree. By definition, University D is the more selective of these two choices.

This option represents the choice for you to go to a community college first and then transfer to a baccalaureate degree program at a four-year regionally accredited university. This decision makes sense when there are significant financial pressures and you cannot afford to enroll in a four-year college immediately. In this situation, you attend a community college to get the "gen ed" credits and then transfer to a four-year institution to study a major and obtain a bachelor's degree.

Competency testing is known in education as "testing out." Go to the College Board site. http://ficws.com/CLEP Review how to "test out" of subjects you feel you are already competent in. "Test out" means that you take a supervised competency exam. A competency exam is one that demonstrates your proficiency in an academic subject.

These proficiency tests are titled CLEP or DSST. Passing these tests relieves you of the need to take the course, thus saving time and money. You can study independently on your own. When you pass one of these tests, you automatically get the college-level credits for the subject covered in the test.

ACCEPTING OR TRANSFERRING CREDITS

Whether the college/university you are considering enrolling in accepts any credits is another matter entirely. Just because you have the credits does not mean that every university will accept them. You always have to keep in mind that, even though you have earned academic credit, whether the university where you are going will accept those credits is up to that university.

Don't be confused. It is not whether you have got the credits. You do. The issue is that it is where you are trying to use those credits that matters in American higher education. To make it as clear as I can, even though you earned the credits, you paid the tuition, and they are on your official transcript means nothing. Not even the U.S. Department of Education can get those credits accepted elsewhere. It is only the university you are entering that has the authority to grant those credits as being valid toward the degree you are seeking.

In the end, this is one of the reasons there are almost 40 million Americans with lots of college credits and no degree.

MONEY MATTERS

Financial considerations impact the decision right from the start of your college selection process. The best ways to reduce the total cost of a degree include maximizing the transfer of previously earned credits from work, completing competency testing, and first enrolling in a community college to pick up cheaper credit hours in core subjects.

It is more difficult to "just get started" and then try to figure out how to pay for the major at the end than it is to look at the entire education picture at the beginning and make a plan. In fact, the community college option and avoiding the trap of Major 1-> Major 2-> Major 3 (discussed in a previous chapter) are available only at the beginning of your degree journey.

The university you select has a big impact on how much time it will take and how much money your degree will cost. Failure to create a thorough plan can result in the waste of time, money, and worthless unused credits.

Remember, the most important decisions are made with good information at the start, not after receiving a degree at the end. Do the research early. It will pay off handsomely.

ACTION STEPS

- Do the university selection exercises outlined in this chapter based on your career choice from chapter 7 How to Pick the Right Career for You.
- Find the college/university in your state with the lowest tuition cost. Find the college/university in your state with the highest priced tuition.
- Document the courses and credits you have already completed.
- Prepare for and take a CLEP practice test of your choice. http://ficws.com/CLEP-Exams

■   ■   ■

10

WHAT QUALITY MEANS
IN COLLEGE

You are never going to go to Harvard University and earn a bachelor's degree. I know. It's a harsh conclusion that may be a bit hard to swallow, but get over it and get on with your life.

Before you become too disheartened by this dose of reality, let me share some facts about Harvard University. The main reason that I want to share these facts is to help you understand a very important truth about American colleges and universities. That important truth is about the quality of American higher education and what it means to your decision.

But before we go to quality, we need to close the discussion about why you will never go to Harvard. You will never go to Harvard University (Yale or Princeton or any of the other high-prestige American universities for that matter) because they do not want you as a student. There, I said it.

These prestigious universities want the best of the best of high school graduates who are prepared to attend classes on campus on a rigid and fixed schedule of what is called synchronous education, delivered face to face by their faculty. They do not want adults who are unable to suspend their lives to go live on the campus in Cambridge, Massachusetts, or Hanover, New Hampshire (Dartmouth). You already have a life—one that you cannot simply suspend to get an education no matter how important that education is to your future. For you there has to be another way.

And it is here that we get into the quality issue in American higher education. Quality is an important part of your education decision at this point in your life. The problem is that you need a better way to evaluate university quality than merely concluding that Harvard and Yale are the best. They may be the best, but that doesn't help you much with your decision. You are not going there.

One thing of use to you is to learn why Harvard has such high prestige. The reason the institution is held in such high regard is not so much about the institution itself, its facilities, its faculty, the quality of its curriculum, or its world-record endowment of tens of billions of dollars.

It is true that Harvard is rich and serves a rich clientele. But money is not the sole consideration in higher education. The quality of the learning is what is important. Another way to look at it is that education quality is really about how much the learning experience at the institution changes the individual—in this case, you.

So you need to realize that prestige and quality of education are not the same thing. Harvard's prestige is built upon the quality of its students. Because Harvard is Harvard, it is able to recruit the highest-scoring high school graduates into their freshman class. In fact, 95 percent of the freshman class applicants are rejected every year (which is another reason that neither you nor I will ever attend Harvard).

The most prestigious American universities have such high prestige because they are able to screen and select only the elite students from American high schools. These colleges and universities have high graduation rates and a highly selective population of students entering the institution in the first place.

With such exclusivity in selection, it is not surprising that the graduates are so highly regarded. They were highly regarded among their peer group before they went to their super-selective university. They were selected by Harvard University because they had already demonstrated they were at the top of their classes at the time of application for admittance.

This leads us to another interesting and important fact about the education decision you are facing. Keep in mind that the goal here is to help you understand the quality of education portion of your decision, not to overstate the prestigious university marker. The interesting question is why prospective students who apply to Harvard, and their parents, put so much stock in the admission letter they eagerly anticipate getting back in the mail once they have submitted their application.

The acceptance letter from the admissions office of a prestigious university means two things to the applicant and, in many cases, more importantly to the parents of that applicant. The first message to that applicant and the parents is about the students themselves. That letter documents a powerful communication.

To the parent, the acceptance letter means that dear Johnnie or Jenny is, in fact, living up to their parents' personal hopes and dreams for their son or daughter. Hopes and dreams are powerful emotional elements in everyone's life. What the acceptance letter says to the parents is this: "Your son/daughter is one of the chosen few. He/She is among the 5 percent of the best of the best who apply to our institution."

With the acceptance letter the anxiety of the application is removed and the parents are able to brag to relatives and friends about how bright and capable their son or daughter is. *Look, my child was accepted at one of the most prestigious colleges in the world. Here (as they wave the acceptance letter) is the proof that I have been a good parent. My kid has turned out so wonderfully and I am proud.* And rightfully so.

The other issue that goes with the Harvard acceptance letter is a belief that acceptance to the most prestigious and selective universities assures success in the future. The acceptance has become a proxy for lifetime success. This may or may not be true, but it is often a belief held at the time.

Of more importance to you is what happens when the application letter comes back as a single sheet of paper (you can tell what it says even before opening the envelope): "Sorry but your application for admission has not been accepted."

Aside from the severe disappointment at the moment, the challenge at that point is to figure out what to do next. In many ways, this is exactly where you are in your decision process, right now. Never mind that you never formally applied to Harvard in the first place; the fact is that you have not been accepted to go to Harvard.

The bottom line is that the quality gold standard of American higher education is not an option. The difficulty is that, like millions of other Americans looking for a quality education, you have to find some other approach to weigh the quality of the institution in your current decision.

The sad fact is that once you get beyond prestige and selectivity, there is little of substance to base a decision on. So let's identify those important facts, explain why they are potentially useful as you make a decision about quality, and give guidance on how to use this information in your search. Here is the short list.

ACCEPTANCE RATE

What is the percentage of applicants to a university who are actually admitted and deemed qualified to attend? This acceptance rate is the indicator of selectivity of the institution. We have already seen that for Harvard this number is around 5 percent. For open enrollment colleges, there is no selectivity. They admit everyone who is qualified to attend.

What does this mean for you? It means that the students in your study group will likely not all be of world-class intellect in an open enrollment institution. Given that you are likely to have study assignments that involve others in your class, don't count on your classmates to be a great contributor to your learning experience. Some will be, but given the open enrollment there are no guarantees.

You prepare for this by accepting the fact as reality (some students just aren't the brightest and may not be helpful to you) and work to find and collaborate with fellow students who can be trusted to make a contribution to your learning.

Not having the guarantee of world-class classmates does not remove the potential for stimulating peer-to-peer learning experiences. It simply means that guarantees of Harvard selectivity are not present in your fellow students. The challenge for you is to find brighter bulbs to work with. They will be there. You just have to find them and team up.

GRADUATION RATE

This is a more important piece of data than acceptance rate. The graduation rate as a percentage shows how many of the students entering a particular university actually are awarded their degree—in other words, how many are successful at earning their diploma.

The important data point here is not the number of graduates, but the percentage of those who entered who completed—most often within six years of starting. The graduation rate at Harvard is 97 percent (yes, wow). The graduation rate at Gonzaga University is 82 percent while at East Georgia State College the student body is 96 percent low income with a graduation rate at 7 percent.

The relationship between income and college performance is a completely different conversation. For now we are merely comparing graduation rates.

What does this mean for you? If you were to look at graduation as a game of chance where the result is a probability based on the past occurrences, a high graduation rate means that you are more likely to graduate than you would if you were to go to a low graduation rate institution.

Going back to the Harvard example, what the 97 percent graduation rate means for you is that you would have a high likelihood to graduate from Harvard if you were to go there. Why? Because you had all of the necessary assets at the time of the original admission. Could you graduate from East Georgia State College? The answer is likely yes. But this is a discussion about quality.

The conclusion about quality is in the combination of acceptance rate and graduation rate. Schools with a relatively low acceptance rate and a high graduation rate means that the school is attracting high-quality students and the curriculum and programs during the education are successful at motivating those students to complete their work. Here, graduation is an indicator of motivation and as such an indirect measure of the quality of instruction that goes on within the classrooms at that institution.

These two rates (acceptance and graduation) are an indication of the quality of the student body (the peers you would learn with and from) and an indirect measure of curriculum quality. The latter is an indicator that the classes are sufficiently motivating and perceived as valuable enough to keep the students engaged to the end. The graduation factor is an important indicator with degree completing adults where the demands of the degree program are competing for their precious time and energy in an increasingly demanding world.

In addition, with adult learners like you, the money to attend most often comes from personal assets. If the school work is not perceived as being worth their time, energy, and money, students do what you would do. They drop out of school or go somewhere else. In the end, graduation rate may not be a bad indicator of education quality, especially where the classes are made up largely of busy adults.

Valuable information source: For quality data on acceptance and graduation rates, see Tuition Tracker, http://www.tuitiontracker.org.

ACTION STEPS

- On Tuition Tracker, for the universities you are interested in, look up the actual tuition paid by the lowest income students.
- Look up the graduation rate for the largest public university in your area. Do the same for the largest private university.
- Set your own standards for what you need from the university you plan to attend. Do the exercise for acceptance rate and graduation rate.
- Ask a friend or relative what university other than Harvard or Yale that they would consider academically prestigious and why.

■   ■   ■

11

HOW TO PAY FOR COLLEGE

T o this point, the focus has been on who you are, your career, your life purpose, how to select a university, and how to reduce your education costs. These are major decisions. Even after you have made all of these decisions, you still face this question: "How do I pay for this investment?" The issue of payment comes after the other decisions, not before. This is why this chapter is at the end of this book, not the beginning.

Many times money issues get moved to the beginning of the decision-making process. It becomes a barrier—something that stops you from achieving your goal. The critical shift here is to approach the money and resources as a means to creating the future you want for yourself and your loved ones. Once you recognize resources as an enabler, not a barrier, you will be able to get what you need to create that better future.

There are many resources to help finance your future. Finding them involves two steps:

- Research the amount and type of financial support available through various institutions and personal resources.

- Use that information to determine the overall investment and return you will receive from earning your degree.

As you look at the costs and the opportunities that exist at a variety of schools, your options will become clearer. By doing some comparison shopping, you will be able to calculate the value you will receive for earning your degree and what your investment will be to accomplish that goal. As a society, we tend to ignore value and cost when it comes to education.

THE MARKET DEMAND FOR COLLEGE GRADUATES (*WILL THERE BE A JOB WAITING FOR ME WHEN I GET MY DEGREE?*)

As with any market, the price (salary you can get) for a degree depends on supply and demand. Without demand, there is no value for holding a college degree. However, the demand for earning a college degree is on the rise. Accordingly, a variety of independent sources are involved in meeting the future needs of our country.

The Lumina Foundation, the leading foundation focused exclusively on policy issues in American higher education, has set a goal of 60 percent of Americans earning their college degrees by 2025. There's no question about it; this is an ambitious goal. In 2011 the percentage of adults with an advanced degree in America was less than 40 percent. This means that millions of degrees must be earned in a relatively short time to achieve the Lumina Foundation goal.

THE BILL AND MELINDA GATES FOUNDATION ESTIMATES THERE WILL BE A NEED FOR 20 MILLION ADDITIONAL DEGREE HOLDERS BY 2020.

Many others are calling for a more educated workforce. The Bill and Melinda Gates Foundation estimates there will be a need for 20 million additional degree holders by 2020. In addition, an independent study conducted by McKinsey & Company concluded that the American economy will need a million more bachelor's-degree holders *every year* through 2020.

While these forecasts may be subject to considerable debate, we know that with the retirement of the Baby Boomers, there will likely be a major shortfall in the supply of degree holders. Baby Boomers are now leaving the American workforce at the rate of 10,000 per day.

Economic theory teaches us about the relationship between supply and demand. When supply is inadequate to satisfy demand, the market makes adjustments through price. In this case, the price is the average salary for degree holders. If the supply falls short, as predicted with the mass exit of Baby Boomers, the market will react by raising the price (salary) to bring supply and demand into balance.

That's good news for you. Employers will be willing to pay higher market prices (salaries) to fill critical positions. They'll have to. Although there are no guarantees, these are the broad market dynamics that will set price.

RISING TUITION COSTS

The job outlook is positive if you want to invest in completing your degree. The resource challenge now becomes paramount as the traditional sources of funding are drying up. For public state universities, the primary source of funding has been state tax revenues used to subsidize the cost of higher education delivery. Resulting tuition prices in public institutions have been below the full cost of delivery. This arrangement worked to the advantage of students and state residents.

States are becoming more strapped for funds, and the result is steep increases in tuition price, even for in-state residents. As a result, costs have shifted dramatically from state taxpayers to enrolled students—potentially, you.

Therefore, the cost of a degree in America has increased rapidly. From 1979 through 2011 the tuition at American universities has increased 1,120 percent compared to an approximate 600 percent rise in health care costs and 200 percent in the consumer price index.

A reduction in tax funds for tuition puts severe financial pressure on students. On the one hand, as we have seen, jobs for degree holders are likely to provide more income for them in the future. Unfortunately, the current job market makes it difficult to have the cash today to invest for the possible return tomorrow.

New sources of investment funds are needed to create the million new degree holders that our economy requires. McKinsey & Company estimates that it will take $52 billion of new funds each year to fund these new degree holders. With pressure on both federal and state funding sources, funding has to come from other sources.

One of the best sources for new capital are the tuition assistance benefits of private corporations. Forward looking employers are willing to pay part or all of the costs of college education for employees they want to develop and retain. In the end, your employer might be the very best option you have to get help financing your education.

YOUR EMPLOYER MIGHT BE THE VERY BEST OPTION YOU HAVE TO GET HELP FINANCING YOUR EDUCATION.

Why would companies be willing to do this? Because they believe well-educated employees help the organization perform better. For more details on this research, go to Bellevue University's Human Capital Lab.
http://ficws.com/Human-Capital-Lab

EMPLOYER TUITION ASSISTANCE

Your current employer might actually be your very best source of capital to pay for your degree. In 2012, non-financial corporations in America had over $2 trillion of cash on their balance sheets. Corporations already were spending a great deal of money for training and education for their employees.

The American Society for Training and Development estimated that in 2010, American corporations spent

$171 billion for employee training and development. This includes tuition assistance dollars that are part of an employee benefit package. The research firm Eduventures estimates that about $16 billion of this total was for tuition assistance benefits to employees. For working adults, this pool of funds represents a significant source of money to help finance degree completion.

Verizon Wireless, for example, spends over $50 million in tuition assistance annually through their highly innovative program called LearningLINK. Through this program, Verizon Wireless employees can attend accredited universities and receive up to $8,500 per year in tuition benefits. Verizon Wireless clearly is investing in their most important asset—their people.

Both the company and the employee have an interest in using those resources for their mutual benefit. The expenditures represent a form of joint investment for both parties who both desire to ensure their investments are productive.

The specifics of tuition assistance benefits vary from company to company, but there are several aspects that apply to almost every company offering this benefit. For the employee, the benefit applies to all employees in a particular class. For instance, hourly unionized employees may have negotiated the benefit in their collective bargaining agreement. Within that same company, the salaried employees may be covered by a different set of tuition assistance benefits. In both cases all of the employees in each group qualify for the benefit.

Check with your manager/supervisor and your human resources department for the specifics regarding tuition assistance that may be available to you. If the financial resources are not currently part of the company's benefit program, you might want to suggest to your leadership that

it would be worthwhile to consider implementing such a benefit. For evidence to support your case, go to Bellevue University's Human Capital Lab.
http://ficws.com/Human-Capital-Lab

OTHER SOURCES OF FUNDING

POST-9/11 GI BILL AND OTHER RELATED PROGRAMS

If you are a veteran, the Post-9/11 GI Bill provides financial support for education and housing if you served at least ninety days in the military after September 10, 2001. Some former military members who were discharged with a service-connected disability after thirty days may also be eligible. You must have received an honorable discharge.

Typically, this bill provides up to $18,077.50 yearly tuition benefits for three years. For the individual veteran, these benefits, including living and book allowances, can total over $79,000 of money available to support their education. The Department of Veterans Affairs administers additional educational assistance programs.

Both veterans and active duty personnel may qualify for more than one of the following programs:

- Montgomery GI Bill (Active Duty and Selected Reserve)

- Reserve or Veterans Educational Assistance Program

- Educational Assistance Test Program

- Survivors' and Dependents' Educational Assistance Program

- National Call to Service Program

- Veterans Retraining Assistance Program

Additionally, free education and vocational counseling services are available. For more information on the GI Bill, go online to the Department of Veterans Affairs. http://ficws.com/GI-Bill

PELL GRANTS

Pell Grants are federal funds for low-income students. They are available to use at approximately 5,400 participating institutions of higher education. Pell Grants are not loans. They do not have to be repaid. The amount awarded depends on the student's financial needs, tuition at the selected school, whether the student is a full-time or part-time student and whether the student plans to attend the school for a full academic year or less.

The maximum award for the 2011–2012 year was $5,550. Student must apply for these grants by completing the Free Application for Federal Student Aid (FAFSA). The U.S. Department of Education has more information on Pell Grants. http://ficws.com/Pell-Grant The Federal Student Aid site is where you go to complete the FAFSA. http://ficws.com/FAFSA

STAFFORD LOANS

Stafford loans are fixed-rate federal loans provided to students attending college at least half time. They offer flexible repayment terms and are not based on financial need. Some loan rates are as low as 3.4 percent per year. Depending on degree status and years in school, a student may be eligible to borrow up to $20,500 per year. A FAFSA must be submitted to be eligible for these loans. The Stafford loan website has more information. http://ficws.com/Stafford-Loan

Note that Stafford loans cannot be discharged by bankruptcy. You would always owe this money with only rare exception. Therefore, to lower your educational debt, it is important to exhaust all other funding opportunities and only apply for this loan as a last resort.

Many students turn to financial institutions such as banks and credit unions for loans. Private loans have a higher credit score requirement and usually have a higher interest rate. Again, these should only be used as a last resort.

Other Grants and Scholarships

There are numerous grants and scholarships available to adults who earn their college degrees. Many incorrectly believe that these opportunities exist only for traditional college students. Instead, grants and scholarships do not have an age requirement and some are specifically for adult students.

Although searching and applying for these awards can be time consuming, the reward is receiving funding for your education that does not need to be repaid.

One warning: you should never have to pay anyone or any service to search for or apply for any grants or scholarships. If you are asked for money to do this, decline to participate in the search and do not apply for the award because it is most likely a scam.

Here are some reputable websites to begin your search for funding:

- A consolidated online guide to financial aid
  http://ficws.com/Financial-Aid-Guide
  - An independent data source that has been around since 1994 and is currently owned by Monster.com, which is a job posting Internet site.

- CollegeBoard
  http://ficws.com/College-Board-Scholarships
  - A tool to find scholarships, other financial aid, and internships from more than 2,200 programs, totaling nearly $6 billion.

- FastWeb http://ficws.com/FastWeb
  - A suite of college scholarship services by company, owned by Monster.com.

REDUCING COLLEGE DEBT

The amount of financial resources required to earn your degree is directly related to the cost of the education. Obviously, with higher tuition and fees the amount of resources required increases. Examine the total overall expenditure and figure out what your financial situation will be when you complete this educational experience. Invest your time into calculating how much you will have invested and how much debt you will have when the degree is complete. Currently, the average amount of debt at the completion of a bachelor's degree is $25,000 and going up.

CURRENTLY, THE AVERAGE AMOUNT OF DEBT AT THE COMPLETION OF A BACHELOR'S DEGREE IS $25,000 AND GOING UP.

It is possible to reduce and manage this potential debt. If you are a working adult, scrutinize your household budget. Are there areas that can be scaled back or eliminated in order to divert part of your income stream toward paying for your education? This in an investment similar to making a house payment or contributing to your 401k—each produces an enhanced benefit in the future.

If your choice of institution comes with a high price tag to finish the degree, the risk of earning that money back in a reasonable period of time is increased. This is why it is essential to spend more effort at the beginning of your decision process to determine the overall costs of completing your education at each institution under consideration. The answers have significant implications for the costs and risks of earning a college degree.

As you continue on your path to earn your degree, the most important decision you have to make is to answer the life-changing question: "What are you going to do with the rest of your life?" It's about your career, the life you want to lead, the person you want to become, and how you are going to provide for yourself and your loved ones. These decisions will impact your financial status, how much you have to invest in your education, your happiness, and the happiness of those around you. It is about the future that is calling you.

ACTION STEPS

- If you are employed, get a copy of your company tuition assistance policy and read it. If you don't understand the policy, talk to your human resources manager.

- If you are not currently employed, get a copy of the tuition assistance policy at a company you might like to work for and read it.

- Document the maximum debt you are willing to incur to complete your degree. Write it down and discuss it with your family.

- Complete the FAFSA form http://ficws.com/FAFSA. This action is required to get a Stafford loan, and you need to become familiar with what the federal government requires from you to qualify for the money.

- Find two institutions in your area where you could qualify for a Pell Grant. Pell Grants do not have to be paid back. They are "free" money. Because these grants are not available at all colleges, you have to ask the university if they are available at their school.

▪   ▪   ▪

12

ESPECIALLY FOR VETERANS

As a thank you to veterans for their military service to our nation, the citizens of America have provided financial resources to help veterans get an education as they transition to new careers in civilian life. But those additional resources are not sufficient to address all the needs veterans have once they leave active duty. Active duty provided a very organized and structured life, and there were few independent decisions veterans needed to make. Mission and purpose were provided by their unit commanders.

As civilians, this is not the case. Veterans will be on their own, faced with making the myriad of decisions that non-veterans face.

O*NET is an extraordinary resource for veterans who are actively making career and education decisions. Veterans have the training and experience they acquired while on active duty. Some of that can be applied toward a degree. I will say more about this in chapter 9: How to Pick the Right School, which deals with your choice of college or university.

Additionally, if you are a veteran, you probably selected your military duty/career path because that is what you wanted to do. If not, then my recommendation is to go to the earlier section in chapter 8: Where the Jobs Are - Today and Tomorrow—O*NET titled, "You don't have a clue about what you want to do."

MAPPING YOUR MOS TO CIVILIAN JOBS

But let's proceed under the assumption that your military career matched fairly well with what you want to do with the rest of your life. Your goal is to make sure you get the most out of your active duty training and experience in your degree and later in your civilian career. O*NET brings some powerful resources to your decision. Let's look at those capabilities in detail.

Go to the O*NET home page. http://ficws.com/ONET You will see

In the block on the right titled ATTN: VETERANS, click on Get Started.

You will see

Under the far right section titled "I liked my last job." look in the box that says Find careers like your military job. Click on the up/down arrow to the right of the top box.

Here is what you will see:

Click on the branch you served. I am going to show the path assuming that you were in the Army. When you click on Army, you will see

Find careers like your military job

Enter the name or code of your military
classification. We'll suggest civilian careers
with similar work.

Army (MOS)

Examples: 15W, radio operator

For the example here I entered the example MOS: 15W,
radio operator. [Note: MOS is the Military Occupation
Specialty code that classifies careers in the U.S. military.] You
need to enter your own service code to find your matching
career opportunities. Next is what you should see but with
your branch of service and your classification entered in the
box below the Army (MOS) box:

MY NEXT MOVE FOR VETERANS

Find careers like your military job

Enter the name or code of your military
classification. We'll suggest civilian careers with
similar work.

Army (MOS)

15W, radio operator

Examples: 15W, radio operator

Click on the **Find** button. You will see

Click on Radio Operators. (Note: This is just to make sure that you understand the site navigation. You should be following your own path for the careers that are of interest to you.) You will see (comparable for your selected career)

At the bottom of the Radio Operators page, you will see

On this page are several important sections to observe and base your next actions on. Remember, this information is based on your going straight into a civilian career as a radio operator. The EDUCATION section shows that little additional education is required for the active duty background of a 15W radio operator in the Army. Unfortunately, the JOB OUTLOOK indicates that the career opportunities in this field are below average, and the average salary per year is $42,080. It is at this point that you need to consider your degree options to have a better career outlook and a higher salary.

You can return to the careers listed in your original search. Simply click on the back arrow on your browser one time and you will see (using our example)

JOBS YOU MIGHT QUALIFY FOR (BUT DIDN'T THINK OF)

Let's assume that you want to get your degree in a career that builds upon your radio operator experience. There is a list of careers that have similar personal characteristics and personality features. You can search related careers with a Bright Outlook For this example I selected Management Analysts. Click on Management Analysts and this is what you will see at the bottom of the Management Analysts page:

This career requires a bachelor's or master's degree. However, there is a growing need for individuals with these skills, and there is a considerable increase in annual income over radio operator. The average salary in 2012 was $78,600 versus $42,080 per year for the less educated radio operator. The path of the discharged 15W radio operator formerly in the Army using his or her GI benefits to earn a degree and qualify for a more positive career prospect and the potentially higher income requires investment of time and money into a degree. So, while the MY NEXT MOVE section gives a summary of these career options, there is much more detail available with another search.

Go back to the home page. http://ficws.com/ONET Click on **Find Occupations**. In the first section titled Keyword or O*NET-SOC Code, enter Management Analysts. Click on **Go** and you will see

Click on 13-1111.00 Management Analysts and you will see

This page contains all of the specific details about a new career for a veteran who was a 15W radio operator in the Army while on active duty. Below are the critical career attributes for Management Analysts as well as the specific career options you are exploring based upon your active duty experience and training.

From this point you need to review the earlier sections of the previous chapter to explore industry and related career options, matching career characteristics and selecting a major for your degree.

ACTION STEPS

- Review your eligible veteran's education benefits at the website of the U.S. Department of Veterans Affairs. http://ficws.com/GI-Bill-Benefits

- Connect with at least two of your active duty buddies who have gone back to school and find out what they have learned.
- Contact at least two veteran-friendly universities from the list at this non-government and non-military-affiliated website.
  http://ficws.com/Military-Friendly-Schools
- Review the list of most military-friendly employers for potential career opportunities. View the full list of the top 100 employers at this non-military website.
  http://ficws.com/Military-Friendly-Employers

■　■　■

13

INNOVATIONS IN HIGHER EDUCATION – WHAT'S NEW

There is a brand new addition to the education market. A new way to take courses is called Massive Open Online Courses or, as they are commonly called, MOOCs (and pronounced *MOO-ks*).

These courses are *massive* because of the number of students who can be taking a single course offered at one time. One course from a former Stanford University professor had 160,000 students enrolled in one section when it was first offered. If you are a bit suspicious about being in a single course with 159,999+ of your "best" friends, you should be. But we will return to this later.

Open means that anyone can enroll—yes, even a ten-year-old or someone who has flunked out of seventh grade.

Online means delivery over the Internet. And *courses* means what we all know courses to be, namely, learning exercises with reading materials, lectures, videos, practice exercises, homework, fixed scheduled delivery with a defined length of study and the opportunity for discussion with fellow classmates.

Missing are such educational conventions as quality standardized assessments (what you might have known as tests in your days in school), admission requirements, full faculty engagement in assignments, and advising.

These unconventional offerings are rapidly attracting students into this new course model. In this chapter you will read about MOOCs. You need to understand MOOCs, and you need to know how you might include them in your journey to your college degree.

In early 2013 MOOCs were offered free of charge. Yes, that's right, at no cost to you. The good news is that you can take a MOOC course without paying anyone anything. All you need to be able to do is log onto the Internet. The benefit is that you can gain access to some of the best curriculum in the world delivered over the Internet for free.

MOOCS OFFER A WIDE RANGE OF COURSES

Elite universities including Stanford, MIT, Duke, Harvard, Berkeley, Penn, Caltech, Brown, Princeton, Johns Hopkins, Rice, Wesleyan, and others totaling thirty-three universities were offering MOOCs in early 2013. A sample of curriculum covered includes

- Biology and Life Sciences
- Computer Science: Artificial Intelligence, Robotics, Vision
- Computer Science: Systems, Security, Networking
- Economics and Finance
- Electrical and Materials Engineering
- Health and Society and Medical Ethics
- Information, Technology, and Design

- Mathematics
- Music, Film, and Audio Engineering
- Social Sciences
- Business and Management
- Computer Science: Programming & Software Engineering
- Computer Science: Theory
- Education
- Food and Nutrition
- Humanities
- Law
- Medicine
- Physical and Earth Sciences
- Statistics, Data Analysis, and Scientific Computing

As we explore MOOCs, you might want to look at a couple of MOOCs through edX and Coursera. http://ficws.com/EDX; http://ficws.com/Coursera

I believe that MOOCs will become increasingly important over time, primarily because many Americans cannot afford the current cost of American higher education. For this reason, as well as their use today, I am introducing them to you here in *Your Future Is Calling*. Over time you should return to this book's website to get the latest on the MOOC developments. http://futureiscalling.com/

In the meantime, I want to bring you back to today. Here is what you need to know right now about MOOCs and your road map to your degree.

One of the surprising things about what is going on with MOOCs is that the courses are being offered by some of the most prestigious universities in America. It's hard to believe, but these great institutions are offering a few of their thousands of courses for free. Note: This is a few of their courses, but by no means even close to all of their courses.

The good news is that the quality of the courses is high, reflective of the quality of the universities that developed them.

Now you might ask yourself why these great universities would give away their most important assets, namely, their courses for free. Those of us in higher education have asked ourselves the same question. The best answer to date is that this is all a branding exercise for the offering universities. That is, because some of their most powerful competitors have gotten press coverage by offering MOOCs, these prestigious universities feel compelled to do so as well. This theory is that it is all about the peer pressure from other universities.

THE DOWNSIDE OF THE FREE MODEL

Here is something I can tell you about this "free" model. It will not migrate to full degrees. Private universities such as Harvard and Princeton that charge tens of thousands of dollars in tuition fees cannot give away the majority of their courses for free even when they have tens of billions of dollars in endowment. If they do, they will eventually run out of funds.

But these college issues are not your issues. Your challenge is to learn enough about these courses to help you in your journey to your degree. Here is one of the most important things you need to know about these MOOCs being offered by these elite universities. Prior to February 2013, not a single one of the courses being offered as a MOOC is accepted toward a single degree at any university—*including their own.*

We have already talked about the fact that in American higher education, whether any credit is accepted at any college or university for any degree program is totally at the discretion of the university where you are trying to get your degree. I cannot overemphasize this point enough. Just because you have credits, it doesn't mean that you automatically apply them to any degree you choose anywhere.

We have already seen what this means with traditional credits. Just to review, here is a specific example that we have already discussed in earlier chapters. You may have been awarded college credits for courses you took at college A. These are authentic college credits that you have as a personal asset. The problem is that when you go to transfer those valid credits to a degree program at university B to be used satisfy your XYZ degree, it is totally at the discretion of university B as to whether those valid credits will be accepted toward your XYZ degree at university B.

So, at this point, you might be asking yourself, *Why is he bringing this up again? He talked about this already in chapter 9: How to Pick the Right School.* But here is the specific point when it comes to MOOCs. At this date, not a single one of the universities will accept the certificate of any MOOC course toward any of their degrees. This is true *even for the MOOC courses from the university offering the MOOC!*

The logical question at this point is this: *If these courses are so great, why don't they count toward a degree at the issuing university?* The answer to this question is important to you today as you decide how to journey on your path to your degree.

Before we get to the bottom line on this credit issue, there is another point you need to consider about whether you invest in time to study in a MOOC. MOOCs are so new that employers have not had the chance to embrace the learning from a MOOC. I had one employer tell me that these felt like a correspondence course or something from Wikipedia. The implication of this perception is that MOOCs do not yet have the credibility needed in hiring decisions. Degrees do.

If you need further evidence about this important job market reality, simply look at open positions posted on Monster.com. http://ficws.com/Monster When it comes to credentials those ads don't say: "Certificates for ten MOOCs required along with three to five years experience." What those employment ads say for example are: "Master's degree preferred. Bachelor's degree required, three to five years experience needed."

The point here is that college degrees are recognized as familiar credentials that employers can use to select potential employees. One could argue that in the end having a particular degree may or may not be valuable. I am a prime example. It's hard to imagine how the majority of my undergraduate physics degree courses directly benefitted me in writing for you here. Oh, I am sure the discipline of solving differential equations for energy transfer problems helps me think logically about things. But I do not see a single sentence in this book with Heisenberg's theories related to hydrodynamics of turbulent flows, the atomic nucleus, cosmic rays, and subatomic particles.

THE UPSIDE OF THE FREE MODEL

The question you have to be asking at this point is, *If courses I take in a MOOC are not worth college credit, what good are they to me?* The answer is that the courses are a good way to learn about a subject that you might want to use in your work in the future. Or, of more immediacy, a MOOC might be valuable to really learn a subject that you are having difficulty with in your current studies. A math course is a good example.

Let's say you have to take algebra as one of your "gen ed" courses to earn your degree in pharmacy. Let's further assume that you have always had trouble with math and stats courses and you dread fulfilling the requirement. Here is one MOOC in particular that could be of immense value to you.

Let's take a look at a unique institution offering MOOCs called Khan Academy. http://ficws.com/Khan-Academy

At the Khan Academy you can get small, subject-matter-specific lessons on just about any subject you might imagine. For example, let's say you are having trouble with one of your least favorite subjects—algebra.

Here I am going to share a little personal secret—at some point in their academic careers almost everyone has had some kind of trouble "getting" a complex math or science subject. This includes me. Mine was statistics. Even with all my math and science, stats did not come easy for me. Why? I really have no clue. All I knew is that it was not like all of my other math experiences, including calculus and differential equations. For a good friend of mine, a senior military officer and a certified engineer, the killer subject was trigonometry. He just could not get it the first time around.

The point is that almost everyone eventually has some personal challenges when it comes to math and science courses. The bottom line is that they are just plain hard.

Here is another little secret about math and science subjects. You absolutely positively have to know inside and out what the words mean. There is no hedging here. In a social science course it might be okay to "get by" with sort of, kind of, maybe sometimes knowing what a term or phrase means. Math and science are totally different. In algebra, for example, it is not good enough to know that in the equation Y=aX+b that these are merely letters standing for something. You have to know that Y is the dependent variable and X is the independent variable and that a and b are constants. Further, you have to know (not sort of know) the difference between a variable and a constant.

But enough about specifics of an equation. We are talking about MOOCs so let's turn to the Khan Academy where they have some important help for you when you are taking the algebra course required for your degree. A MOOC at Khan Academy to the rescue!

Go to Khan Academy's math site. https://www.khanacademy.org/math/algebra-home   Here you will find all kinds of free lessons on an important assortment of algebra topics including

- What is a variable?
- Evaluating expressions in one variable
- Expressions with two variables
- Evaluating expressions in two variables
- Examples of evaluating variable expressions

Notice that the lessons are broken down into small, digestible chunks. The other important point about the Khan Academy is that the lessons are free and you can take any course as many times you need to. I know of one case where someone working on his degree just could not "get" a particular subject. Comprehension was difficult, and as a result, he wound up taking that particular Khan Academy lesson thirty-six times! He stayed with it until he got it. Bravo!

My advice about the Khan Academy is to use the lessons as very targeted tutorials to help you learn about a specific topic or subject, especially if you get stuck as all of us do from time to time. This advice is especially important when it comes to STEM (Science, Technology, Engineering, Math) courses where it is especially easy to get lost.

This brings us to the end of this summary exploration of MOOCs. They are out there. They have some use today, but you have to know what they are, where they are, what they have to offer, and, above all, their limitations. They have use to you today and they will become ever more valuable in the future. Learn and use them wisely.

MOOCs do not change anything that you have read in this book to this point. You need to start with who you are, select a career, select a college or university, and then learn the material. To earn a degree you will have to demonstrate competency in the subject matter of the courses. MOOCs will not allow you to avoid examinations, papers, or other familiar forms of academic assessment, but you will still have to demonstrate that you know the subject matter and can think critically about the issues in the course.

Until early 2013, the structure of MOOCs has not had the accredited assessment as a part of their design. This is the barrier to credit awarding that I alluded to earlier. What has emerged are third parties authorized to assess the learning and assign college credit for successful completion of the assessment.

The American Council on Education (ACE) is leading the way on the development of ways to assign academic credit to MOOC courses. In February 2013 they recommended academic credit for four MOOC courses. It was inevitable that more followed. A whole new fork in the yellow brick road to a degree is rapidly being built, and you need to know about it. That is what this chapter has been about.

ACTION STEPS

- Access and take two lessons at Khan Academy in two different subjects of your choice. Take notes.

- Look up and review the requirements for a Coursera course of your choice from Duke University.

- Compare and contrast a Coursera course from Stanford with a MOOC from Harvard.

- Go to edX and learn how to register for an upcoming MOOC course.

- For your chosen career(s) from chapter 7: How to Pick the Right Career for You, find five different lessons on Khan Academy that might be valuable in your newly selected career.

■　■　■

14

STAY THE COURSE

In writing this book my goal has been twofold: (1) to provide you with the motivation, inspiration, and drive that will help you complete your college degree; and (2) to identify the critical decisions you will make along the way that can prevent you from getting derailed in achieving your goal.

Having information and determination is the essence of staying the course. It means stepping onto that path toward completing your degree and remaining on it until you create your own future. This is accomplished through a series of data-gathering steps including figuring out who you are, what degree and career fit the vision you have for your life, and how best to implement your commitment to be the best you can be. In other words, staying the course is doing the critical work to achieve your degree that helps you fulfill your dream.

WARNING: ROADBLOCK AHEAD

Unfortunately, getting on the wrong road or veering off course can lead to lengthy delays in completing your college degree. You might experience the all-too-familiar Major 1->Major 2->Major 3 sequence. Or you may decide the school you selected just is not right for you and you have to start all over.

At best, these outcomes are disheartening and discouraging. At worst, they waste precious time and financial resources. In every case they spawn exhaustion, impede dreams, and delay the creation of the future life you are working toward.

When you encounter these roadblocks, reread chapters 3 and 4. Do the Action Steps again. Earning your degree will not happen just because you read this book. You have to do the work. Discover once again who you are and then determine where you got off track on the first attempt or attempts to earn your degree. Finding *your* right path will lead you to your desired future. The major, your career, the university you select are all means to that end.

If you are like most people, you probably skimmed the chapters of this book looking for the "good parts"—the gems of wisdom and new insights. If so, then you probably skipped the Action Steps (the work), especially the detailed effort required in chapters 7, 8 and 9. It is easy to look at the screen shots, get a general idea about what was being said and then move on to the end.

With some books that approach might be sufficient. It is not sufficient here. The examples in this book are just that—examples. They are not about me, and they certainly do not represent exactly what you want for your future. The only way to create your ideal future results from doing the work. Read the information and make the choices based on who you are.

Information is important, but in the end your success will be driven by the emotion you bring to achieving your goal. For you the emotion should be about your contribution to your own future. My wish is that this book helps you create that future.

Keep the image of the life you are trying to create in front of you as you journey on your educational path to your future. From here on, it's up to you.

ACTION STEPS

- Reflect on the two most powerful emotions you had when you began to read this book. What were they? Compare those with the two most powerful emotions you feel now.

- What is your plan now?

■　■　■

SELF-INVENTORY

This self-inventory captures your personal assessment on critical resources that you already have. These are resources that can help you make good choices as you select your learning road map.

It is important that you actually write out your answers. This is where you are taking the inventory on *who you are*. Remember, who you are is the place you start this entire effort to invest in a degree that fits you. After all, this is about *your future*—the rest of your life.

SELF-ASSESSMENT INSTRUMENT

FUTURE VISION

What I want:

_____

When I think about what it means to have my degree my thoughts are about:

Myself   My loved ones   Financial

Career   Other

PERSONAL CAPABILITIES INVENTORY

Personal capabilities scoring: 1 – 10
(Circle the one that most applies to you)
1 = I have little or no capability   10 = I am an expert

Math	1 2 3 4 5 6 7 8 9 10
Reading	1 2 3 4 5 6 7 8 9 10
Writing	1 2 3 4 5 6 7 8 9 10

What I think I would like to be doing every day in my future:

Math	1 2 3 4 5 6 7 8 9 10
Reading	1 2 3 4 5 6 7 8 9 10
Writing	1 2 3 4 5 6 7 8 9 10
Speaking	1 2 3 4 5 6 7 8 9 10
Working with others	1 2 3 4 5 6 7 8 9 10
Working alone	1 2 3 4 5 6 7 8 9 10
Other:	1 2 3 4 5 6 7 8 9 10

_____

Post-secondary education

Schools attended where I need to get transcripts

1.

2.

3.

Financial

Sources I need to investigate

Company tuition assistance

_____

Personal savings

_____

Military benefits

_____

Pell Grants

_____

Scholarships and grants

_____

Student loans

_____

Commercial bank loan

_____

Other

_____

SUPPORT AND RESOURCES

Potential mentors

1.

2.

3.

LEARNING RESOURCES

My activities that could qualify for academic credit

Corporate training

_____

Military training

_____

Civic activity

_____

Work experience

_____

Independent study

_____

CLEP

_____

DSST (college credit exams)
see http://ficws.com/Get-College-Credit

_____

OTHER THINGS I NEED TO KNOW TO MAKE A DECISION

The place I want to study if location is a factor

_____

Other

_____

_____

_____

_____

NOTES:

_____

_____

_____

_____

_____

_____

_____

_____

_____

_____

_____

_____

_____

_____

NOTES:

ABOUT
THE AUTHOR

As the first member of his family to attend college, let alone graduate and go on to earn advanced degrees, Mike Echols knows firsthand the value that a college degree can bring to work, health, happiness, and to life. He also knows firsthand that, without close role models to support a decision to earn a college degree, it can be lonely and at times an overwhelming journey.

After high school, Mike earned his bachelor's degree in physics from Carnegie Mellon University, then went on to earn an MBA from the University of Pittsburgh and Ph.D. from the University of California, Berkeley.

His career began as assistant professor in the School of Business at the University of Wisconsin–Milwaukee. Later his corporate career was at the General Electric Company where he held three senior executive roles. From there, he returned to academia as an entrepreneurial senior executive, first as Executive Director of the Creighton Institute for Information Technology and Management at Creighton University in Omaha.

In 2000 he began work for Bellevue University in Omaha, an innovative university that provided services that made it possible for working adult learners to earn their college degrees—long before most universities even contemplated the need for it. In 2007, Mike was recognized as one of the Top 20 Most Influential Training Professionals in America by Training Industry, Inc.

After publishing three books about corporate learning, *ROI on Human Capital Investment, Competitive Advantage from Human Capital Investment* and *Creating Value from Human Capital Investment,* Mike worked with Bellevue University to establish the nation's first Human Capital Lab, the first academic department dedicated to measuring the value created by corporate learning.

Mike heads up the Strategic Initiatives Division, which created the Human Capital Lab at Bellevue University, where pioneering research is conducted on the return on investment (ROI) from human capital investment in corporate learning. He also leads the Veterans Initiative for Advancement (VIA) designed to help returning young veterans make a successful transition into a productive civilian career.

This body of work is available in trade publications with specific scientific case studies available for download. http://ficws.com/Human-Capital-Lab

His work in Strategic Initiatives and Human Capital Lab has garnered numerous prestigious honors and awards including the "Excellence in Academic Partnerships" Gold Award with partners The Home Depot, Verizon Wireless, SunTrust, Convergys, and CACI. Bellevue University was ranked in the Top Leadership Development programs nationally by *Leadership Excellence* magazine.

Mike's passion for helping adult learners succeed in school—and in life—remains with him. His latest thinking about education and the workplace can be found at his blog. http://www.learnprosper.com

FUTUREISCALLING.COM

**REGISTER NOW TO RECEIVE
FREE PERIODIC UPDATES AND
ACCESS TO ADDITIONAL RESOURCES**

Human Capital LLC

www.ingramcontent.com/pod-product-compliance
Lightning Source LLC
Chambersburg PA
CBHW020201200326
41521CB00005BA/215